how to be a
better....

decision
maker

THE INDUSTRIAL SOCIETY

The Industrial Society stands for changing people's lives. In nearly eighty years of business, the Society has a unique record of transforming organisations by unlocking the potential of their people, bringing unswerving commitment to best practice and tempered by a mission to listen and learn from experience.

The Industrial Society's clear vision of ethics, excellence and learning at work has never been more important. Over 10,000 organisations, including most of the companies that are household names, benefit from corporate Society membership.

The Society works with these and non-member organisations, in a variety of ways – consultancy, management and skills training, in-house and public courses, information services and multi-media publishing. All this with the single vision – to unlock the potential of people and organisations by promoting ethical standards, excellence and learning at work.

If you would like to know more about the Industrial Society please contact us.

The Industrial Society
48 Bryanston Square
London
W1H 7LN
Telephone 0171 262 2401

The Industrial Society is a Registered Charity No. 290003

how to be a better....
decision maker

Alan Barker

KOGAN
PAGE

The
Industrial
Society

YOURS TO HAVE AND TO HOLD

BUT NOT TO COPY

First published in 1996

Kogan Page Limited
120 Pentonville Road
London N1 9JN

British Library Cataloguing in Publication Data

A CIP record for this book is available from the British Library.

ISBN 0 7494 1950 4

Typeset by DP Photosetting, Aylesbury, Bucks
Printed in England by Clays Ltd, St Ives plc

CONTENTS

Introduction   9

1. What is a decision?   15
Defining a decision   15
Thinking about decisions   17
Extending our choice   19
Putting decisions in context   23
Managing the decision making process   28

2. Considering   31
The decision cycle   31
Step 1: Identify the problem   32
Step 2: Generate alternatives   45
Step 3: Eliminate alternatives   49

3. Consulting   61
Consult or participate?   61
The dangers of consulting   64
Whom to consult   65
Consultation by conversation   66
Appointing a consultative team   73

4. Committing   79
Managing objective risk   81
Managing emotional risk   83

5. Communicating   93
Whom to communicate with?   93
Selling the decision   98

Delegation   103
Sharing goals   108

6. Checking **111**
Monitoring performance   112
Following people's progress   124
Developing people   130

Afterword *135*

Bibliography *139*

Index *141*

HOW TO BE A BETTER... SERIES

Whether you are in a management position or aspiring to one, you are no doubt aware of the increasing need for self-improvement across a wide range of skills.

In recognition of this and sharing their commitment to management development at all levels, Kogan Page and the Industrial Society have joined forces to publish the How to be a Better... series.

Designed specifically with your needs in mind, the series covers all the core skills you need to make your mark as a high-performing and effective manager.

Enhanced by mini case studies and step-by-step guidance, the books in the series are written by acknowledged experts who impart their advice in a particular way which encourages effective action.

Now you can bring your management skills up to scratch *and* give your career prospects a boost with the How to be a Better... series!

Titles available are:
How to be Better at Giving Presentations
How to be a Better Problem Solver
How to be a Better Interviewer
How to be a Better Teambuilder
How to be Better at Motivating People
How to be a Better Decision Maker

Forthcoming titles are:
How to be a Better Negotiator
How to be a Better Project Manager
How to be a Better Creative Thinker
How to be a Better Communicator

Available from all good booksellers. For further information on the series, please contact:
Kogan Page
120 Pentonville Road
London N1 9JN
Tel: 0171 278 0433
Fax: 0171 837 6348

For Peter

INTRODUCTION

Good decisions are at the heart of good management.

We are all decision makers. Every aspect of our lives – as managers, family members, citizens – is governed by decisions. Our ability to make decisions – to choose between one thing and another, rather than following blind instinct – is a defining feature, we feel, of our humanity. Whether we work in or with organizations, the quality of our work depends on the quality of our decisions.

Perhaps you feel that you can improve the quality of your decisions, and the way you make them. You may feel that you are too indecisive: that you hesitate too much, that you are too capable of seeing all sides of a question, that you lack courage on occasions to make decisions that you know will be unpopular. On the other hand, you may be aware that some of your decisions are too hasty: that you have a tendency to 'jump first and think later'. You may feel that your background, experience, expertise or education has not fitted you well for the messy business of making decisions.

Managers make things happen. We achieve results through other people. Increasingly, we are being asked to manage *change*: to deal with it, help others to deal with it – and to create it. And management itself is changing. Managers are being given more and more decisions to make, in ever more complicated circumstances.

We tend to think of decisions as events, moments in time with a 'before' and an 'after'. Decisions seem to have a 'point of no return', before which we can revoke or cancel the decision, and after which we cannot turn back. It is this point of no return that can make some decisions so difficult to make: we must commit to a course of action without being able to predict all its consequences.

For decisions are not only events: they are also parts of interrelated processes. They are surrounded by influences and effects, many of which we will be unable to see directly. A decision's context will include:

❑ the patterns of change within which it happens;
❑ other decisions: past, present and future;
❑ the organizational structure;
❑ the views and objectives of other people;
❑ our own experience, objectives, ambitions, fears and emotions.

What is more, our decision will itself affect the context. Its consequences will probably create more decisions in the future. Those consequences are not straightforward matters of linear cause-and-effect. They will ripple outwards in all directions like waves in a swimming pool, affecting people in other teams, departments, divisions – even other organizations. We work in a continually fluctuating wave pattern created by the consequences of our decisions; the waves we make in one part of the pattern can have consequences on the far side of the pool.

Clarifying the boundaries of an issue – the parameters within which we are making a decision – is therefore fraught with difficulty. John Adair identifies three broad categories of decision:

❑ *obvious decisions:* predictable, routine, causing comparatively little dissent or difficulty;
❑ *emergency decisions:* taken in a crisis, at speed, with little time for thought or consultation;
❑ *all the others*.

The Kepner–Tregoe (K–T) method – one of the more well-known 'rational' decision making approaches – distinguishes between:

❑ *problems*, which are defined as deviations from a norm;
❑ *plans*, which are the means of dealing with potential problems;
❑ *decisions*, which are choices between alternatives.

In practice, many decisions will involve solving problems, and making a decision will help to solve a larger problem. Similarly, a good decision will only work if we create a workable plan; and good planning includes the flexibility to make decisions within it. The K–T method is undoubtedly useful in helping us to see what we are trying to do at each moment; but rational decision making must include flexibility, common sense and an ability to live with ambiguity.

Tudor Rickards offers five categories of problem that can usefully be adapted to decisions.

❑ *One right answer decisions.* We tend to look for decisions that do precisely what we want and no more, or to assume that there is one 'correct' course of action. Such decisions exist; but they are rare.

❑ *Insight decisions.* These decisions come to us in a flash. They cut through our habitual ways of looking at issues and our assumptions about what we can do in a situation. Such decisions may not be demonstrably 'correct'; instead, they 'feel' right and have an aesthetic appeal (they provide an 'elegant solution').

❑ *Wicked decisions.* We cannot see whether a wicked decision is the best one until we act on it. The test of the solution is in implementing it ('I think the ice is thick enough; shall we try it?'). Many decisions are of this kind: they require courage, creativity in execution, and a readiness to deal with the unexpected.

❑ *Vicious decisions.* Vicious decisions generate problems for other people greater than the problems they solve. Deciding to relocate a company to a remote 'green field' site may be a good strategic decision for the Chief Executive; it may create nightmares for staff.

❑ *Fuzzy decisions.* Fuzzy decisions have unclear boundaries and cannot be made using solely rational methods. Wicked and vicious decisions are fuzzy; so are most of our larger, everyday, non-technical decisions.

The vast literature on decision making is mostly devoted to helping us make more rational choices. Our thirst – and the frequent demands of senior managers – for measurable results and 'hard' evidence make such approaches apparently attractive. Very few decisions, however, can be well made using logical processes alone.

Ever since Roger Sperry's work on perception in the late 1960s, it has become increasingly fashionable to talk of 'left-brain' and 'right-brain' thinking. 'Left-brain' has come to be associated with the processes of logic, language, reasoning, number, linearity and analysis; 'right-brain' with image making, rhythm, spacial awareness, association and creativity. We even speak of people's thinking style as being 'excessively' left- or right-brain oriented. Although such a model only crudely reflects what research has revealed about the workings of the brain, it has value in reflecting a deep-seated *attitude* to thinking. It seems to make sense to divide our mental processes into two broad categories: 'hard', analytical or 'rational'; and 'soft', intuitive or 'imaginative'.

It may be useful to reflect on your personal style of decision making in these terms. You may favour a strongly logical approach: amassing information, calculating probability and assessing risk in numerical terms. An effective decision, however, also involves less controllable or measurable factors: insight, aesthetic appeal, 'gut feeling'. On the other hand, if you prefer to rely on experience, flair and imagination, you may find it useful to develop your analytical skills to support your judgement and make it more acceptable to others.

It is by *combining* these two broad styles of thinking that we can become better decision makers. This book is designed to help you integrate logic and intuition in your quest for more effective decisions.

Chapter 1 examines what a decision is and the kind of thinking that it requires. It puts decisions into context and introduces a systematic approach using 'the five Cs': Considering, Consulting, Committing, Communicating and Checking. The rest of the book looks at each of these factors in turn.

Chapter 2 – on Considering – introduces the decision cycle, a thinking process involving three steps: identifying the issue or problem; generating alternatives; eliminating alternatives. It also offers a range of tools and techniques at each step. Not every decision will require all of them. Some are focusing activities and will be particularly useful in the context of Total Quality Management (TQM) or process improvement. Others are scanning devices that aim to deepen and broaden our understanding of a problem and help us generate alternative courses of action.

Some decisions will require a more radical approach: systems theory and the creative techniques in this chapter will help us to find new perspectives on an issue and tackle it in innovative ways.

Eliminating alternatives is as important as generating them. Ranking and Rating, and Solution Effect Analysis, will help us sift the feasible solutions from the possible ones, and make a final choice of action.

Most decisions will affect other people in one way or another. Chapter 3 examines the process of consultation, distinguishing it from instruction and participation, and considering the advantages and problems associated with consultative teams.

Commitment is at the heart of decision making. Chapter 4 looks at rational and intuitive approaches that will help us find the necessary belief and enthusiasm to see a decision through.

Many decisions fail through poor communication. Chapter 5 covers the means by which we sell ideas and gain others' commitment. Implementing a decision is primarily a matter of communicating it: this chapter also investigates delegation and gaining the co-operation of other managers to make our decision happen.

Chapter 6 discusses the processes of checking and monitoring our decision and brings us full circle. Checking the effects of a decision is often the first step in considering the next. Decisions are part of the wider learning cycle – execute, review, think, plan – that we all travel in our continual efforts to improve our performance.

There is no such thing as the perfect decision. We can never guarantee that every decision we make will be 'right first time'. Making decisions is a matter of designing solutions, and the test of any solution is in its execution. Making decisions can be a lonely business. *How to be a Better Decision Maker* is intended to give you some friendly help: to be a source of ideas, support and guidance.

Many people have contributed to this book. Numerous delegates on training courses and seminars have granted me insights into their decisions. Ian Hodgson at Barclays Financial Services offered a number of key ideas from a TQM perspective. At the Industrial Society, Jenny Davenport, Andrew Forrest, Brendan McDonagh, Bill Orson and Adam Somerset helped me in various ways. Ron Coleman at Invicta Training, too, was generous with his time and ideas. Michael Wallaczek's work on non-linear results and dialogue management was a particularly rich source of inspiration. Philip Mudd and Gabi Facer at Kogan Page gave consistently friendly support. Peter Bassett, Helen Magee and my wife, Gill, gave their time to help me find clearer ways of expressing my ideas.

My thanks go to all of these people. The decisions about the book's final form and content, of course, were mine alone.

WHAT IS A DECISION?

How good is your decision making? Do you mainly get decisions right or often make bad mistakes? What influences the way you make decisions? Would you make the same decision differently on different days?

You probably do not notice most of the decisions you make. We all make hundreds – maybe thousands – of decisions every day. Decisions are a fundamental part of human activity. Our lives are shaped by decisions; our success depends on the quality of our decisions and on the skill that we bring to making them.Yet how often do we give any thought to the process of decision making?

The actual moment of making a decision is not easy to study. There is something mysterious about it: it can be sudden; we may not be able to explain it. Often we feel that a decision has somehow made *us*.

DEFINING A DECISION

What, then, is this curious event that we find so hard to understand?

Making a decision is committing to a course of action

Making a decision is *more* than choosing what to do. It involves making a commitment, however small: rationally and emotionally. Furthermore, it often involves making a commitment on behalf of others – particularly in a work or family situation – and asking them to commit to your commitment.

As well as commitment, a decision requires *action*. It includes problem solving: indeed, the first step in making a decision may be to clarify the problem to be solved. Both problems and decisions can be of many kinds: technical, administrative, personnel, budgetary. Often, of course, a single decision will involve problems in any or all of these areas! But solving a problem may not necessarily involve *doing* anything; making a decision will always result in action of some kind. This is true even if we decide to do nothing: choosing non-action is as much a decision as any other.

Every decision has consequences

Committing to a course of action is always uncomfortable. There is a 'point of no return', before which it is possible to revoke our decision, and after which we are truly committed. Some decisions, of course, will have a number of key commitment points, with the costs of changing your mind rising as you pass each. Such decisions start soft and slowly 'set', like cement; it can be difficult to identify the precise point of no return.

Passing that point takes us into unknown territory, for the effects of a decision will always be unpredictable. Some of them may be invisible to us. Other people will probably be affected – whether they share our commitment or not. If we make a wrong choice, we may be able to undo it; if our commitment falters, a lot more may be at stake: our reputation, people's trust in us, our own self-esteem – maybe the future well-being of our team or organization.

Every decision is provisional

Perhaps the most difficult aspect of committing to a decision is that decisions are never final.

A decision is the best choice of action we can make at the time. It will almost certainly be adjusted, overturned or superseded – maybe in the very near future. How can we honestly commit to something so temporary?

THINKING ABOUT DECISIONS

Most of us would agree that a good decision is a well-informed decision: that, before making it, we have considered all options, covered every aspect and understood every implication. Making a well-informed decision requires 'rich thinking'.

And yet most decisions are made with little real thought. Consider the thought that went into your last visit to the supermarket. How well informed was your last business decision: to write up your monthly report for your manager; to send a standard letter to a customer; to spend half a day sorting out a technical problem that you might have easily delegated to one of your team?

A number of prejudices seem regularly to hinder the thinking that precedes decision making.

All questions in business are essentially simple
Simple – or simplistic? Is the problem a simple matter of cause and effect? Or part of a complex system of interrelated processes? And if the question involves people – as most managerial questions do – it is unlikely to be simple.

It is all about the bottom line
This usually means money. But using the phrase 'the bottom line' may be an excuse for sloppy thinking. Where is the bottom line? How do we calculate it? Whose bottom line? How many bottom lines are involved? Which should we consider? Who decides where to draw it? When is it drawn?

All decisions are short term
'Why bother thinking too much about it? Everything will change tomorrow anyway.'

This is a misunderstanding of the idea that all decisions are provisional. Of course the future is uncertain; that is no reason to refuse to think about it or plan for it. We need to think about even the smallest business decisions in terms of our longer-term objectives. If we have no course set, we are reduced to reacting to things as they happen: the 'firefighting' that characterizes so much organizational decision making.

We know what we are talking about

It is all too easy to make facile assumptions about the context of a decision: the organizational habits that dictate our behaviour; the restrictions on resources, personnel or budget; the consequences of any action; the way competitors will respond. If we allow ourselves to be the prisoners of our assumptions, we are more likely to be taken by surprise.

If we want better results, we need to make better decisions. And if we want to make better decisions, we had better improve the thinking that goes into them.

We must begin to see thinking as an essential management tool. We are paid to think. Good thinking does not depend on intelligence: intelligence by itself achieves nothing. Neither does it depend on education: many highly educated people find it difficult to think well. Thinking is not the accumulation of information: good thinking recognizes that the information available can never be complete.

So why do we not give more consideration to the quality of our thinking as managers?

'I haven't got time to think.'

'Change is ever more rapid; all of us are under pressure. Our thoughts will be overtaken by events before we know it.'

A manager with no time to think is a manager who will perform poorly. Management is primarily about thinking: if you are not paying attention to your thinking responsibilities, you are probably not organizing your time effectively. And remember: we can think at the speed of light. Maybe what we need to do is improve the *quality* of our thinking.

'I can already think.'

'Thinking is what I do naturally: it is no more than the application of common sense to specialized data.'

We are not taught to think about thinking. As a subject on the curriculum, it does not exist. No wonder, perhaps, that we give little consideration to the way we manage our decisions.

'Thinking never gets us anywhere.'
'Thinkers' – people who think for a living – are notoriously impractical. Business – particularly in a fast-moving environment – seems to demand rapid reactions, intuitive responses, seizing the main chance.

On the other hand: where does *not* thinking take us?

'I'm not paid to think, but to get things done.'
We tend to place thinking and action as polar opposites. In truth, we are paid to get results. We think when we want to achieve a result that is better than it would be without thinking.

Some organizations systematically degrade thinking. They may develop a 'macho' culture in which thinking is seen as effete or weak – a sign, indeed, of indecisiveness. The 'best' decision maker is seen as the 'fastest gun'. Others value 'busyness': working as long as possible, humming with electronics and making every decision on the run. How many of the decisions in such organizations are truly good ones? How much time do executives spend making excuses for a decision that turned out badly?

EXTENDING OUR CHOICE

Making a decision involves choice. If we are not choosing to do something, we are not truly deciding. Choosing can only happen if we have alternatives from which to choose. And we can only find those alternatives if we take the trouble to look for them.

The two stages of thinking

We can imagine thinking as a process in two stages:

perception; judgement.

In the first stage, we look at reality and name what we see. We find a way of talking about it: we turn reality into a language. In the second, we make sense of reality by manipulating the language.

We are very good at second-stage thinking. We are trained in the process of logic and argument, we are educated to manipulate languages. We can even build machines to do second-stage thinking for us: computers are second-stage thinking devices.

We are not nearly so proficient at the first stage; so weak is our command of perceptual thinking that we hardly think of it as thinking at all. Without pausing to examine the accuracy or form of our perceptions, we 'leap to judgement'.

Improving our decision making depends, not only on improving our second-stage thinking, but on enriching our perceptions at the first stage. Good logic applied to poor perceptions will produce poor results: in computer talk, 'rubbish in: rubbish out'. If our perception of a situation is narrow, our ability to decide what to do will be dangerously limited. Only by broadening and deepening our perception will we be able to generate genuine alternatives for action.

The great Swiss psychoanalyst, Carl Jung, developed this two-stage model into two pairs of complementary mental functions: *sensation* and *intuition* as functions of perception; *feeling* and *thinking* as functions of judgement.

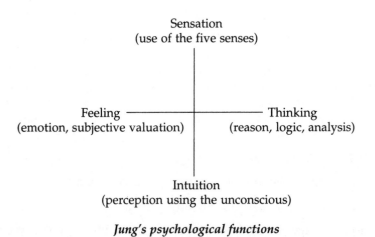

Sensation
(use of the five senses)

Feeling ——————————— Thinking
(emotion, subjective valuation) | (reason, logic, analysis)

Intuition
(perception using the unconscious)

Jung's psychological functions

Sensation is perception using the five senses; intuition is perception using the unconscious. Our senses give us information about immediate reality; intuition helps us see the reality that lies beyond the immediate: deeper relationships, patterns and potential.

Intuition is perception of the possibilities inherent in a situation.

Carl Jung

Thinking – in Jung's terms – is rational judgement: giving meaning to what we perceive by using logic, analysis, argument. Feeling is value judgement: using emotion, morality, ethics or aesthetics to evaluate what we see as pleasant or nasty, good or bad, beautiful or ugly.

All four psychological functions are at work when we make decisions. Our senses help us to see reality clearly so that we can act on it; and thinking – logical reasoning – is at the heart of rational decision making. We are also strongly governed by our feeling function, particularly when decisions involve other people or when commitment is difficult.

Rational decision making, however, may ignore the vital role that intuition has to play. If intuition is perception of the possibilities of a situation, it will be of great value in helping us estimate the potential consequences of any decision we make, as well as helping us perceive our circumstances more deeply.

Without doubt, we use our intuition constantly as managers – though some of us may feel uncomfortable admitting it. And, as with the other three mental functions – sensation, thinking and feeling – we can use intuition well or poorly. The problem, of course, is that intuition uses the unconscious: we perceive something as potentially true without knowing *how* we come to know it.

We cannot consciously summon an intuition. We can, though, help to prepare for intuition, to make it welcome when it calls. Chapter 4 discusses this idea further.

Designing solutions

Most people are promoted to management on the basis of their:

❏ expertise;
❏ experience.

We use both kinds of thinking to increase our understanding of our situation. Expertise involves thinking about specific areas of knowledge. Experience allows a manager to apply knowledge about particular areas of work.

Thinking for decisions uses both our experience and our expertise; but its purpose is different.

Decision making is a *design* process. Designing solutions is like designing tables: there can never be a 'right' answer. The table's design will depend on: its purpose; the resources, time and skills available to us; and our current knowledge of how tables work best. Making a decision, similarly, depends on: why we are making it; our available resources, time and skills; and our understanding of the situation. The very best decision we make will only ever be the best at the time.

Action not truth
We are not thinking to find the truth, but to get something done. Action thinking cannot be done in isolation: it must involve applying our thinking in the world, testing it in practice. It will probably involve thinking with other people.

Consequences not causes
Such thinking involves prediction, the calculation of probabilities (not certainties) and the balancing of risk against reward.

Future not past
Making a decision is part of a plan for the future – including contingency planning for what might go wrong, and even for what we cannot foresee.

Results are provisional
The success of a decision will depend on circumstances over which we have little or no control: other people, wider systems and procedures, policies and drivers for change emanating from elsewhere in the organization, events in the world beyond. We can never know everything about the context of a

decision, nor about its possible consequences. Making decisions is what John von Neumann calls 'a game of imperfect information'.

PUTTING DECISIONS IN CONTEXT

A decision's effectiveness depends on the context in which we make it; and that context is dynamic: it changes over time.

Many factors will affect a managerial decision: our objectives, the objectives of our team or department, the strategic objectives of the organization, other people's objectives, the way the market is moving, legislation, policy decisions.

Event or process?

A decision is usually seen as an event. But it is also part of numerous processes: procedures, systems, the consequences of other decisions. In particular, a decision forms part of a continual managerial process: the learning cycle.

We decide on the basis of past experience: how could we do anything else? Yet we are choosing a course of action for the future. And the future is never like the past. Hence the need for a continual cycle of thinking and learning.

Making effective decisions becomes even more difficult when the consequences of the decisions are not immediately obvious: if we cannot see them, if there is a delay before we become aware of them, or if they occur in another part of the organization (or within a larger system within which the organization operates).

> *We learn from experience but we never directly experience the consequences of many of our most important decisions.*
>
> Peter Senge

Decisions will be based on our review of previous decisions, on our thinking and planning to meet future objectives. The decision itself, of course, changes the context in which it was made and will influence later decisions. Even not making the decision will affect the context. 'Doing nothing' may be an option; but it is as much a decision as any other.

Ownership

Who should make the decision? Ownership is critically important if the decision is to be successful.

Decisions, it is generally agreed, should be taken at the lowest possible level of authority and the highest possible level of competence. It makes sense to delegate decisions as far down the line as we can; but the decision to do that is itself sometimes tricky.

> *The charge of the Light Brigade was ordered by an officer who wasn't there looking at the territory.*
>
> Robert Townsend

In order to make a decision, you need:

❑ authority;
❑ resources;
❑ skills.

You may not truly 'own' the problem: it may be somebody else's difficult decision, 'offloaded' on to you. More broadly, you may lack elements of authority that continually hamper your ability to take ownership of decisions.

HOW MUCH AUTHORITY DO YOU HAVE?

Every manager must have limits to their authority if an organization is not to go completely out of control. Have you agreed with your manager where those limits are? Have you agreed with your team or subordinates the limits of their authority?

Personnel decisions

Are you authorized to:

- ❏ increase staffing levels?
- ❏ recruit and select staff?
- ❏ reallocate people or tasks?
- ❏ set pay levels?
- ❏ handle grievances?
- ❏ issue verbal or written disciplinary warnings?
- ❏ dismiss staff?
- ❏ negotiate with trade unions or employee representatives?
- ❏ give references?

Financial decisions

Are you authorized to:

- ❏ operate a budget?
- ❏ give discounts?
- ❏ allow credit?
- ❏ invest the company's money?
- ❏ obtain credit or borrow on the company's behalf?
- ❏ authorize rental or lease agreements?

Technical decisions

Are you authorized to:

- ❏ purchase?
- ❏ set the limits on your purchasing?
- ❏ appoint, terminate or negotiate with suppliers?
- ❏ agree or change specifications?

Continued on next page

> *Continued from previous page*
>
> ❏ set quality standards?
> ❏ subcontract work?
> ❏ initiate legal proceedings?
>
> If you are not sure of your authority in any of these areas, your ability to make decisions may be hampered. Discuss the matter urgently with your manager.

Ownership may be fudged or unclear. Different people may own:

❏ the problem;
❏ the decision;
❏ the solution.

If those people fail to work well together, they will tend to make bad decisions.

CASE STUDY

When is a good decision a bad decision?

Simon, a team leader on a development project, responds to an increase in workload over several months by advertising for a new team member. He sees six candidates, picks one and offers her the post. That afternoon, his manager tells him that a strategic decision has been taken to pull the plug on the whole project. Simon has to contact the successful candidate and withdraw his offer.

His decision was a good one, based on his knowledge at the time. It was a bad one – wasteful, appalling PR for the company, humiliating – in the context of other decisions over which he seemed to have no control.

Such lack of communication between managers may be symptomatic of a wider inability in the organization to encourage good decision making.

Your ability to own the decision will also be affected by the wider culture of your organization. Most organizations (or parts of an organization) can be placed somewhere on a continuum between 'risk-averse' and 'risk-hungry'.

Risk-averse	Risk-hungry
bureaucratic	'liberated'
process-oriented	customer-oriented
control of input	control of output
predictable	innovative
obedience	commitment
conformity	initiative
maintaining adequacy	pursuing excellence
consistency	continuous improvement

In a risk-averse organizational culture, you may be allowed to make only a limited number of decisions; others must be sanctioned or approved by higher levels of management. In a risk-hungry culture, you will be empowered to make as many decisions as possible, and be given the skills, resources and support to make them.

To make a decision in a risk-averse organization, you will need:

❏ to know how your decision will be affected by other parts of the organization;
❏ the ability to compromise or subordinate your judgement to that of others;
❏ knowledge of the precise limits of your authority;
❏ the ability to 'play the system'.

To make a decision in a risk-hungry culture, you will need:

❏ access to all the information you need to evaluate your situation;
❏ the self-confidence to trust your own judgement;
❏ the authority and skill to act quickly and effectively;
❏ the ability to work in teams.

Of course, organizations rarely conform exactly to one or other type of culture. Indeed, parts of a single organization may be relatively liberated while others remain hopelessly bureaucratic.

TAKING OWNERSHIP

Use this checklist to help you take ownership of a decision and recognize the limits of your authority.

Background

How has the need for the decision arisen? What needs to be done? Why? What is the context?

Responsibility

Why are you involved? Where does it 'hurt'? How does it affect you personally? What motivates you to find a solution? What does the problem 'feel' like?

Past efforts

What has already been tried? Have other recent decisions led to this one? Has anyone had to make such a decision before? Is this decision a second try?

Authority

What are you in a position to do? What resources are at your disposal? What are the limits of your authority? What are you willing to do? Who else is involved?

Ideal solution

A big wish. If miracles could happen, what would you ask for? What would be the best possible decision? What is your vision of the future after the decision is made? Wish for the impossible!

MANAGING THE DECISION MAKING PROCESS

As managers, we probably spend most of our time thinking: in meetings, in corridors, at lunch, on the phone, travelling, at rest, in bed, while watching television, while exercising.... What can we do to develop this most crucial of our managerial skills?

A systematic approach can be extremely useful. It can ensure that:

❑ we do not leap to conclusions;
❑ we have a 'map' of our choices;
❑ we have a clear means for evaluating them;
❑ we can explain our thinking more clearly to others;
❑ we can record the process if necessary;
❑ we prioritize and set realistic targets.

A systematic approach cannot guarantee a good decision; but it can weigh the odds in favour of one.

Research among many managers has suggested a basic framework for the decision making process. In the real world, of course, no situation will ever match the framework exactly; but almost every managerial decision can be expected to conform to it more or less.

The 'five Cs' of decision making – considering, consulting, committing, communicating and checking – are factors in the process, not steps in a procedure. We will often be engaged with more than one factor at a time: consulting while considering, communicating tentatively before committing, checking a previous decision as part of considering the next.

Considering
Identifying the alternatives; exploring the alternatives; eliminating the alternatives.

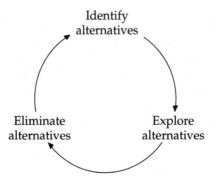

Considering is iterative: a process we may need to repeat several times. We may have to use the decision cycle several times before we arrive at a decision that satisfies us.

Consulting

Involving those affected: in exploring the issue, in making the decision, in implementing the solution. Distinguishing between consultation and participation. Using others to enrich our own thinking, in conversations and meetings. Appointing teams as part of the process.

Consulting often forms part of considering.

Committing

At the very heart of the process. Taking responsibility for the decision: managing the external and the emotional risks of the decision. Finding our own inner commitment. Making it real by announcing the decision.

Communicating

Explaining what you have decided and why. Implementing the decision by generating commitment from others. Selling the benefits and securing action. Delegating and planning.

Checking

Monitoring progress to ensure that the decision actually works. Using performance indicators and modifying plans in the light of progress. Walking the job to review and encourage. Reviewing the decision as part of the learning cycle and preparing for the next decision!

Making a decision is much more than taking it. Like it or not, no decision will be successful without the co-operation, commitment and enthusiasm of your colleagues, team or customers. How often have you heard a manager say: 'Taking the decision is easy – the hard part is getting others to commit to it'? Many a decision has been unsuccessful because of this confusion: a manager has seen their responsibility as deciding what to do and then simply announcing it.

Management is about getting results through others. Making a decision involves making it happen.

2

CONSIDERING

Making a decision begins when we realize that something needs to be done. It may be clear what that is; it may only seem so. We may have been told to do something, but not how; we may be completely surprised by a turn of events that forces us to decide quickly.

THE DECISION CYCLE

The purpose of considering a decision is to *generate choice*. Only with a real choice can we make a real decision. We need to think, and to structure our thinking.

Considering is not a straightforward, linear process. It is far more useful to think of it as a cycle, to be repeated as often as necessary. The cycle has three steps:

1. identify the problem;
2. generate alternatives;
3. eliminate alternatives.

There are four principles that are important in following it.

The cycle is a **design** *process.* We are designing a course of action. There is no 'correct' answer; only better or less good solutions. We may need to go round the cycle several times before we achieve a decision with which we feel happy.

The whole process is important. We must go through every step if the decision is to have a chance of being effective.

31

Each step involves the two stages of thinking. At each step, we must carefully look at the situation and develop our perception of it, before evaluating, judging and choosing.

The process needs to be managed. This is especially true if others will be involved in the thinking process (as they almost certainly will be).

STEP 1: IDENTIFY THE PROBLEM

Our purpose at Step 1 is to look more fully at the problem. Only by enriching our perception of it can we begin to generate genuine alternatives for action.

Our very first move must be to create a preliminary picture of the problem in our mind.

IDENTIFYING THE PROBLEM:
a preliminary checklist

What?

What is the problem?
Can we break it into parts?
Does one part have priority over others?
To what other problems does this problem relate?
What is the background to the problem?
How big is the problem: large, medium or small?
What will happen if the problem is not solved?
What will happen if the solution is delayed?

Why?

Why has the problem arisen?
Why did we not recognize the problem before?
Why has the organization not tried to solve it already?

Continued on next page

Continued from previous page

When?

When did we first notice the problem?
Is the timing of the problem significant?
Is it a recurring problem: regular, seasonal, part of a pattern?
By when is a solution needed?
Does the problem have to be solved in stages?

How?

How was the problem first noticed?
How does it affect our performance?
How has it been dealt with before?
How could we go about dealing with it now?

Where?

Where does the problem occur?
Is it confined to one area (department, site, outlet, function)?
Is the problem local or global?
Is the location of the problem significant?
Does the problem occur elsewhere?

Who?

Who owns the problem?
Who first noticed the problem?
Who was responsible for the problem occurring?
Who is most or worst affected? Who would own the solution?
Who would most benefit from the solution?
Who needs to be consulted?
Who owns the decision?

Try to formulate a *problem statement*, defining the problem as exactly as possible. Identify:

❏ initial conditions: where you are now;
❏ goal conditions: where you want to be;
❏ operators: how you might achieve your goal conditions.

Problems are more or less well structured according to how exactly we can describe these three factors. A well-structured problem can be tackled using clear operators: thinking techniques, action plans, targets, milestones and measures of progress. An ill-structured problem will need to be tackled differently: maybe limiting it in order to create a more well-structured problem, changing the parameters within which we try to tackle it, or taking a more creative approach.

A technical problem, for example, is probably well structured. Correcting a fault in a machine or a piece of software involves a clear sequence of operations resulting in clear goal conditions: we will know unambiguously when the fault has been corrected. Improving a working relationship with another person, on the other hand, is a very ill-structured problem: we may not be able to say precisely what is wrong, nor what would make it right. Finding clear operators to solve such a problem would be difficult.

PARETO ANALYSIS

Pareto analysis is a very simple way to separate the major causes of a problem (the vital few) from the minor ones (the trivial many). It is based on the 80/20 rule: the idea that 80 per cent of problems are due to 20 per cent of causes.

The Pareto diagram is a bar chart where classifications are arranged in descending order from left to right. The only exception is a class called 'other', which, if used, is located on the far right.

Pareto is useful for:

- ❑ displaying the relative importance of contributing causes to a problem;
- ❑ breaking broad causes into components;
- ❑ choosing a starting point in tackling the problem;
- ❑ creating a focus on causes in priority order;
- ❑ comparing the effects of action: 'before' and 'after'.

Continued on next page

Continued from previous page

1. **Decide what data to chart.** What is the effect you want to improve? What are the contributory factors to that effect?
2. **Decide how the data should be classified.** Identify possible causes for failure or shortfall, or types of problem. You could classify by:

   - ❏ production shifts;
   - ❏ types of defect;
   - ❏ reasons for lateness or mistakes;
   - ❏ type of stock or part.

3. **Collect data over a specified period.** Take care to collect data that fits exactly into each category.
4. **Summarize the data.** Arrange the data in descending order; total the data across the rows; calculate percentages.

Reasons for customer complaint

	Frequency	Cumulative frequency	%	Cumulative %
Faulty goods	104	104	51	51
Faulty packaging	68	172	33	84
Price error	11	183	5	89
Wrong addressee	10	193	5	94
Late delivery	6	199	3	97
Poor service	3	202	2	99
Faulty invoicing	1	203	1	100
Failure to refund	1	204	1	

5. **Draw the diagram.** Plot the data, remembering to put the longest column on the left.

Continued on next page

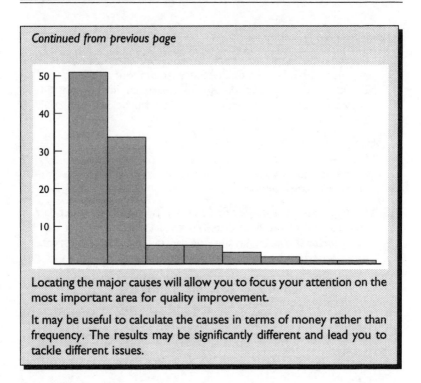

Continued from previous page

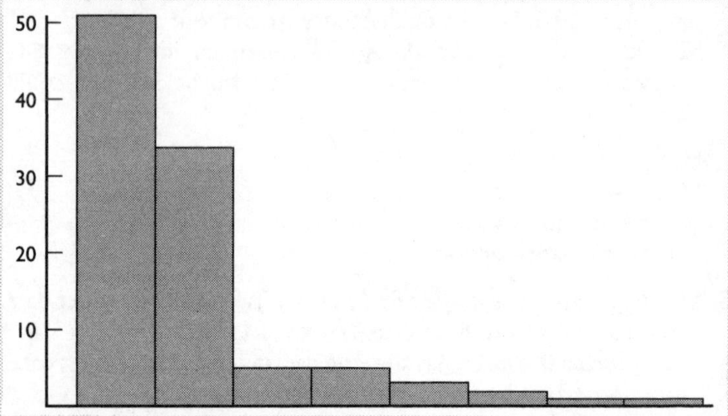

Locating the major causes will allow you to focus your attention on the most important area for quality improvement.

It may be useful to calculate the causes in terms of money rather than frequency. The results may be significantly different and lead you to tackle different issues.

As well as clarifying problems structurally, we can distinguish between *presented* and *constructed* problems.

Presented problems

What is a problem? Our first answers would probably suggest obstacles in our path:

- something that must be solved (removed/minimized/ignored);
- something that cannot be solved (removed, etc...);
- something we are set;
- something that causes pain or stress;
- something we would rather not have.

Such problems are presented problems. We had no part in creating them; we may feel no responsibility for them. They prevent us getting where we want to go. They tend to create stress.

We might characterize a presented problem by using the phrase 'whether to...':

❑ a piece of machinery breaking down: whether to mend it or not;
❑ a target set us by somebody else: whether to aim at it or not;
❑ a professional relationship breaking down: whether to end it or not;
❑ a sudden shift in interest rates: whether to change our financial strategy or not.

Presented problems severely limit our thinking. We are faced immediately with a clear choice: 'whether to ... or not'; 'either/or'. This can be very helpful: the lack of choice may help to 'make the decision for us'. Indeed, the aim of using the decision cycle may be to resolve the matter down into such a simple, two-way choice.

Sometimes, however, it may be extremely difficult to commit to a choice when we had very little control over the problem. Our decision may be little more than a caricature of a decision if:

❑ we do not own the problem;
❑ we are looking at the 'wrong' problem;
❑ we are only looking at a part of the problem;
❑ we have been given authority but insufficient resources;
❑ we are constrained by policy or legislation;
❑ we have been allocated resources but insufficient authority;
❑ we are constrained by our lack of skills or expertise;
❑ we know that we will not own the solution.

We may be constrained, too, by our assumptions and prejudices about a problem. It is worth asking some hard questions early on.

❑ What is the real problem?
❑ What evidence do I have? Do I have any contrary evidence – to support a view different from my own?

❏ What is my objective? What is my immediate aim? Is it in line with my longer-term objectives?

❏ Is my objective in line with the broader objectives of my team, department, division or organization?

❏ What action would most effectively help me toward my objectives?

❏ Where am I now?

❏ Am I trying to close a measurable gap?

❏ Do I know how to close the gap?

❏ Will I know for sure when I have solved the problem? How?

Such questions will help us question our narrow choice of options (or our apparently narrow choice).

FISHBONE DIAGRAMS

Fishbone diagrams help to make cause and effect analysis more sophisticated. In situations where the causes of a problem cannot be measured, or where the issue is complex, fishbone diagrams help to clarify the major issues and links between contributory factors.

Fishbone diagrams were invented by Professor Kaoru Ishikawa of the University of Tokyo. The method is sometimes called the Ishikawa Method.

1. **State the problem.** Place the problem statement in a box on the right-hand side of a large piece of paper.
2. **Draw a horizontal line across the paper, to the left of the problem box.**
3. **Ask: 'Why is the problem occurring?'** Place each reason on a line running at 45° from the main stem – like the ribs on a fish's backbone.
4. **For each reason, again ask: 'Why?'** Add each new reason as sub-stems to the appropriate branches.
5. **Identify linkages.** Some reasons and sub-reasons may be closely linked. Others may appear more than once.

Continued on next page

Continued from previous page

Fishbone diagrams allow us to:

❑ focus on an overall problem rather than on parts;
❑ find more than one cause, countering the illusion of a simple cause–effect relationship;
❑ escape from 'squirrel-caging' – obsessive attention to a part of the problem;
❑ ponder the issue over time;
❑ see the linkages between causes clearly;
❑ discuss the problem in a team or group;
❑ generate new ideas;
❑ counter possessiveness of ideas in group decision making;
❑ establish a logical sequence of actions for tackling the problem: plans, priorities, etc.

One of the most exciting developments in the last two decades has been the growth of systems thinking in management. As management has become subject to ever more unpredictable change, many theorists and managers have sought to understand the patterns underlying events, rather than focusing on the events themselves. The models they have developed can be useful in gaining new insights into complex problems and making decisions about how to solve them.

The ideas originated in cybernetics, the study of communication and control processes in biological systems (such as the nervous system or an ecosystem), mechanical systems like engines, or electronic systems such as computers. Thinkers such as Chris Argyris and Peter Senge have applied them fruitfully to social systems such as teams and organizations.

The foundation of systems thinking is the idea that every event is part of a larger system of processes and relationships. The system itself is subject to two kinds of feedback: reinforcing feedback that accelerates the development or growth of the system by reinforcing its initial conditions (the way that an amplifier works); and balancing feedback that arrests the system's development and maintains a state of equilibrium (a thermostat, for example, maintains an optimum temperature by turning a heating system on and off).

Both kinds of feedback operate as *cycles*. The key to understanding systems theory is to see that events are parts of cycles rather than the linear effects of individual causes. Increased publicity for a product, for example, can result in sales growth, which itself creates greater public awareness and so pushes sales up still further.

This reinforcing cycle will, however, not allow the system to grow indefinitely. As sales grow, plant will reach capacity and the company will be unable to meet demand. Sales will be limited by production capacity and a balancing cycle will come into play, linked to the reinforcing cycle. The upturn or downturn in sales – the events as monitored in sales figures – are subject to the workings of these two cycles of activity.

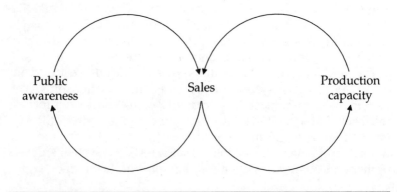

Peter Senge has named this pattern 'limits to growth', and has called it an 'archetype' because it is so common in industry.

Systems thinking places decision making in an entirely new context. No longer are we to look for causes of effects; instead, we are encouraged to examine the larger system within which a problem is occurring, and ask how we might intervene in the system to weaken or remove the problem.

Such intervention is called *leverage*. In looking for points of leverage, we are looking for actions that will influence a whole network of relationships and influences, rather than alleviating a symptom.

❏ Distinguish symptoms from underlying causes. How do the causes interrelate? What reinforcing or balancing cycles seem to be at work?
❏ Take care not to do what was done in the past. Previous solutions to the same problem, if they have failed, have probably only been 'quick fixes' – addressing events rather than processes, symptoms rather than the underlying dysfunction.
❏ Identify points of leverage. Where in a cycle could you intervene? What would the consequence be to the system as a whole? Where else could you intervene? How?
❏ How could you strengthen the whole system?

Constructed problems

What is a problem? Pondering the question further, we might add some more definitions:

❏ something that *can* be solved;
❏ something we set ourselves;
❏ a challenge;
❏ something that gives us the opportunity to do better;
❏ a catalyst.

Constructed problems are challenges that we set ourselves. The problem did not exist before we created it. There may be nothing wrong; we are interested in the possibility of improvement, or change, or doing something different.

Constructed problems give us no clear choice of alternatives. A range of possibilities is available. In decision making terms, we can express a constructed problem as a phrase beginning 'How to...':

❑ gain a qualification;
❑ improve our performance;
❑ innovate a new product;
❑ increase our market share;
❑ improve an existing procedure or service;
❑ develop a strategy.

The defining feature of a presented problem is a discernible gap between what is and what ought to be. The defining feature of a constructed problem is a created gap between what is and what could be.

It may be possible to translate a presented problem into a constructed one. Such a translation:

❑ gives us ownership of the problem;
❑ transforms an obstacle into a challenge;
❑ allows us to see the wider context of the problem;
❑ opens up the possibility of choice;
❑ helps us to generate alternatives.

Making such a translation is, of course, itself a decision! It may be unnecessary. On the other hand, it may be useful in helping us towards Step 2 of the decision cycle, in which we will be generating alternatives for action. Above all, it can transform our attitude to a difficult or intractable problem – a problem that resolutely remains ill structured, for example – and reawaken our determination to tackle it.

'How to'

The easiest way to convert a presented problem into a constructed one is to cast it as a 'how to' statement.

❑ whether to repair the machinery:
   how to repair the machinery

❑ whether to aim for a target set by somebody else:
how to meet the target

'How to' immediately suggests possible courses of action: 'I might...'. Each is a potential decision. Each 'how to', moreover, itself suggests new 'how to's'.

❑ how to repair the machinery:
  ❑ how to get the machine working
  ❑ how to use only part of the machinery
  ❑ how to get the job done without using the machinery
  ❑ how to maintain productivity
  ❑ how to stop getting stressed
  ❑ how to satisfy demand in some other way
  ❑ how to replan the schedule
❑ how to meet my target:
  ❑ how to counter the effects of adverse trading conditions
  ❑ how to work smarter not harder
  ❑ how to save time/money/resources
  ❑ how to manage my time more effectively
  ❑ how to exceed my target

The range of 'how to's' deepens and broadens our perception of the problem, preparing us to generate more alternatives at the second stage.

Backwards planning

This is a useful technique for clarifying goals. By regarding the initial 'How to' as a solution rather than a problem, we move backwards, asking what higher-level problem it might solve. We can repeat the process with the new problem, and so on.

Higher-level 'how to's' will be more general than the original; they will also bring our personal aspirations into clearer focus.

Take a 'How to' statement and ask:

❑ 'If I achieve it, what will that give me?'
❑ 'And if I had *that*, what would it give me?'

Try to focus at each level on benefits to you, rather than anybody else. Ask:

❑ 'If I had that, would I want it?'
❑ 'Might there be any other way of achieving it?'

To take an example:

How to increase business with existing key accounts by 10 per cent over the next quarter.

'If I achieve it, what will that give me?'

More business! Actually, more solid business, more stable relationships.

'And if I had *that*, what would it give me?'

More time to develop the relationships: less time chasing business.

'And if I had *that*, what would it give me?'

Greater power to plan.

'And if I had *that*, what would it give me?'

The opportunity to improve what I do.

Our range of constructed problems now includes:

❑ How to increase business with existing key accounts by 10 per cent over the next quarter.
❑ How to build more stable relationships with my key customers.
❑ How to find the time to develop relationships with key customers.
❑ How to spend less time chasing new business.
❑ How to be able to plan more effectively.
❑ How to improve what I do.

Repeated backwards planning will expose broader objectives, putting our decision into context and helping us to identify priorities.

Before long, you will be faced with an array of 'how to' statements. You will need to choose which to pursue.

Ask:

❏ What is my objective?
❏ What is my broader objective?
❏ How do immediate objectives relate to broader ones?
❏ Which takes priority?
❏ How would solving this problem help achieve them?
❏ Do I own this issue? Do I have authority, resources, abilities?
❏ Is there a genuine choice/lack of clarity about this?

Remember that, by the end of Step 1, our goal is a 'How to' statement that will trigger new ideas for action. We are not aiming for 'whether to' until the very end of the cycle.

STEP 2: GENERATE ALTERNATIVES

The purpose of Step 2 is to generate possible courses of action. It is potentially the most creative part of the decision cycle.
 What stops us from exploring alternatives?

❏ *Lack of time*
 Some decisions have to be made 'on the spot'; but very few are literally split second. A very few moments exploring possible course of action can save untold difficulties later. This part of the decision cycle cannot be forced. If you feel under pressure of time, it may be more important to find ways of relieving the pressure rather than leaping to a decision.

 How much time do you actually have – in hours, minutes and seconds? Why do you feel under pressure?

> *A man that cannot sit still in his office . . . and that cannot say no . . . is not fit for business.*
> Samuel Pepys

❏ *Being defeated by complexity*
 There can be a real fear that we will be overcome by the possibilities that we unleash by generating alternatives.

 The real danger, however, is that we will limit our alternatives unnecessarily. It is far better to manage the process of idea generation than to ignore it. Be prepared to sift possibilities at the end of Step 2: to refer them to your wider objectives, prioritize alternatives and put some 'on hold'.

❑ *A dislike of waste*
Generating ideas will inevitably mean that all except one will be rejected later.

Deliberately creating waste probably goes against the grain. But it is essential if we are to make a good decision. Remember, too, that rejected ideas may have their uses later, in other contexts. It can be useful to record all your ideas: to store them for recycling rather than throwing them away.

❑ *Risk to our reputation*
Expressing incomplete ideas is often ridiculed in organizations. We may feel that our image will suffer if we show ourselves to be 'indecisive': that we will be treated with intolerance, hostility or even contempt. Maybe we are not encouraged to indulge in 'alternative' thinking; better perhaps to keep our heads down or 'toe the line'. Perhaps we risk making enemies by thinking 'outside the square', or starting rumours and misunderstandings. We may need to think privately.

How, then, to go about thinking at Step 2? What kinds of thinking will help to generate the possible courses of action we are looking for?

Gathering information

Good decisions require good information. Information is 'the solar energy of organizations': without it, all our work would grind to a halt.

Information helps us see the bigger picture, and the finer detail. However, as information becomes ever more accessible, complex and more easily manipulated, there is a real threat that we can begin to worship information at the expense of good thinking.

Information is the shape of our thinking. It is only as useful, therefore, as the shape of the thinking that created it. Information can never be complete: it grows and changes with time. The dangers are that:

❑ we could go on gathering information for ever;
❑ we may only gather the information we're looking for (in order to justify a conclusion or decision we want to make);
❑ we may become overwhelmed with information.
❑ we may confuse facts with interpretation;
❑ we may interpret facts inappropriately or illogically.

> *When the facts change, I change my mind. What do you do?*
> John Maynard Keynes

Being creative

Creativity involves breaking mindsets: the mental patterns by which we interpret what we see. We can use a number of techniques to help us see the problem in different ways and reveal new potential ways of dealing with it.

Rule reversal
Look for the 'hidden persuaders': the rules that govern your thinking. Identify any procedures, systems, habits or conventions that must be observed to accomplish a plan of action. Now reverse them or eliminate them: maybe you will reveal a new alternative.

For example: to hire a new member of staff might require placing an advertisement in a public journal. Reverse the rule: how about advertising your organization to potential candidates? How about trying to put people off applying?

How do these absurd ideas suggest new ways of advertising the post?

Metaphorical excursions
Imagine your problem existing in another, completely unrelated field. Suppose a supply chain were a food chain in the natural world? Suppose reorganizing an administrative

system were like steering an oil tanker? Suppose improving your relationship with suppliers were like baking a cake?

How would you solve the problem in this metaphorical world? What analogies could you make with the real situation?

Using an oracle

Oracles introduce a random element into our thinking, that knocks us out of our mental habits. By 'force-fitting' a connection between two apparently unrelated items, we provoke a new thought.

Throw dice to generate a random sequence of numbers. Use the sequence to identify a page, and then an individual word, in a large dictionary. Ask what possible connection there may be between your problem and that word. Concrete nouns and verbs work best. If the word you land on is an abstract concept, try moving on to the first concrete noun or verb following.

'How/How' thinking

'How/How' thinking is a useful tool for generating alternative courses of action. It is, in essence, backwards planning in reverse!

Begin with a 'How to' statement and imagine you have chosen it as your preferred course of action. Now ask how you could implement it: identify a small number of actions. For each of them, in turn, ask how they can be achieved. After three or four stages, a number of 'chains' of action have been worked out, at a greater degree of detail at each stage.

You can draw a 'How/How' diagram to display the pattern of alternatives. This allows you to:

❑ see alternative courses of action clearly;
❑ sift the possible from the impossible;
❑ identify recurring possible actions;
❑ work out courses of action as rough plans.

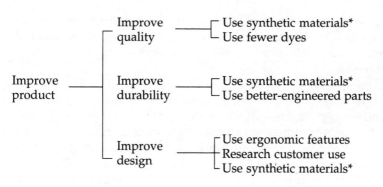

* One course of action shows three times: it is a possible solution.

STEP 3: ELIMINATE ALTERNATIVES

Our purpose at Step 3 is to resolve all our alternatives into one clear choice: *whether to...; either* this *or* that.

Our thinking at Step 2 has left us with many possible courses of action. We must now sift the feasible from the possible.

Scan the options before you quickly, identifying those that are feasible given your current:

❑ authority;
❑ resources;
❑ abilities.

From a small number of alternatives, we can proceed towards a final choice by elimination. How many options you choose to evaluate in detail will depend on available time and your own intuitive appraisal of which options are attractive. Three or four are probably enough.

If you cannot decide immediately which option to pursue, you must submit yourself to the rigour of objective evaluation and, if necessary, the discipline of numbers.

Managers often resist this kind of thinking. We are, after all, judging the effectiveness of action in the future. And the future is uncertain. Why bother thinking about it, let alone preparing for it? The danger is that we can easily find ourselves in a vicious circle: uncertainty makes it useless to think or plan; lack of thought or planning makes the situation even more uncertain; and so on. This mental paralysis is a common cause of indecisiveness.

Being able to break that paralysis is often seen as a matter of 'character' rather than skill. 'Belief' takes over from judgement, and making the choice becomes a matter of creating that belief. A situation's 'enormous potential' blinds the decision maker to the 'negligible risks', and before long they have convinced themselves that a 'probable success' has become 'virtually guaranteed'. In the absence of cool thinking, hotter emotions can all too easily take over. In an organizational culture that values action over thought, intuitive and rapid decision making may be praised as courageous – or even 'manly' – and those who urge caution are derided for their cowardice, disloyalty or lack of 'spunk'.

But we can evaluate probability and risk. Indeed, actuaries, meteorologists and bookmakers make a living out of it! Anybody selling insurance solely on the basis of 'intuition' or 'gut feel' will soon find themselves out of a job. All decision makers must be prepared for mixed results; but effective thinking at this stage will tip the odds in favour of a good decision and against the possibility of a bad one. The only way to handle uncertainty well is to assess it objectively.

Elimination of feasible alternatives is a matter of taking each option and:

❏ appraising it against established criteria;
❏ considering the possible consequences of implementing it.

Appraisal criteria

Appraisal criteria can help us choose between alternatives. It often helps to itemize and record our criteria of choice, in order to make sense of complexity and to help us justify our decision to others.

A simple method of assessing a course of action is to make a straightforward list of 'pros and cons', in two columns down a page. Edward de Bono has developed this tool into a three-way appraisal, listing positive, negative and interesting aspects of an idea.

It is important to use a tool of this kind in a systematic way. Look deliberately for positive, negative and interesting points, in that order.

Positive points are whatever makes the idea attractive. Ask: 'What are the benefits? What extra benefits are there?' Include your own feelings as well as objective advantages.

Negative points are the weaknesses, shortcomings, risks and dangers associated with the idea. They are presented problems. Transform them into constructed problems by creating a 'How to' for each one. A single negative point can suddenly become a dozen potential ideas for improving the original idea.

Interesting points are implications, consequences, effects on other people or systems, potential by-products or spinoffs. What might the decision lead to? What else might happen?

RANKING AND RATING

Ranking is the structured process of placing options in order of preference. Rating scores the options against pre-selected criteria.

Ranking and Rating helps us to choose between possible courses of action, and to prioritize alternatives in order to use resources most effectively. It is commonly used to select candidates for a job; it is useful for any decision where selection criteria can be accurately identified.

1. **List the options.** Be as precise as possible; keep the number of options manageable.
2. **List the selection criteria.** Remember that the choice of criteria will fundamentally affect the final decision. Make the list before evaluating the options.
3. **Categorize the criteria** as either 'essential' or 'desirable'. An 'essential' criterion should be one against which an option can only 'pass' or 'fail'. Desirable criteria can be weighted according to desirability (most desirable being, say, 10).

Continued on next page

Continued from previous page

4. **Test the options against the essential criteria.** Any option which 'fails' any of the essential criteria can be eliminated.

5. **Rate the remaining options against the desirable criteria.** Having weighted the desirable criteria out of 10, score each option against those criteria up to the total weighting value of that criterion.

Add up the scores for each option. The highest rated emerges as the preferred option.

Companies making major investment decisions or seeking to improve their processes may use a large number of criteria to choose a course of action. They may use computers to calculate weightings and scores. One of the dangers with Ranking and Rating is that we can be seduced into measuring everything, rather than focusing on key criteria or performance indicators. Many projects collapse, for example, under sheer mass of numbers: measurement takes priority over judgement.

Assessing the consequences

Making a decision will result in action. That action will take place in the future. Assessing the possible consequences of a decision is therefore of the utmost importance.

In assessing consequences, we are thinking in terms of probability. Some consequences will be certain to happen (100 per cent probability); others may seem completely unlikely (0 per cent). Most will be less easy to put a number to. All will be impossible to quantify exactly. This doesn't mean, however, that we shouldn't try. Putting a number against our assessment is an excellent discipline.

It is also important to assess consequences in terms of time: immediate, short term, medium term and long term. The proportions will vary from decision to decision. Managers (and organizations) can be notoriously obsessed with short-term results; selling the long-term benefits of a decision may be fraught with difficulty.

There are two fundamental calculations of probability to be made:

❑ the probability of success;
❑ the balance of risk against reward.

Estimating the probability of success is a matter of asking:

❑ What could go wrong?
❑ How likely is it to happen?

We must take care to look for factors external to our decision that may affect it: events over which we have no control. In particular, a decision that relies for its success on an external event (an upturn in the market; a competitor going bankrupt; the exchange rate moving in a particular direction) is highly risky.

Managers might not like to hear that a decision has only a percentage probability of being successful. We would all prefer to deal in certainties. You will have more credibility as a decision maker, however, if you can quantify the probability of *failure* and show how you plan to deal with it.

If you estimate that your decision has an 85 per cent chance of succeeding, what factors lead you to assess the chances of failure at 15 per cent? Itemizing them is the first step in making contingency plans to deal with them. Making those plans effectively reduces the chances of serious failure and boosts the prospects for success.

Assessing the balance of risk against reward is a different, but no less vital, calculation. Your decision may have an 85 per cent chance of succeeding, with a consequent 20 per cent improvement in profit, productivity or efficiency. If the cost of failure, however, were a 60 per cent loss of profit, productivity or efficiency, is the risk worth taking?

SOLUTION EFFECT ANALYSIS

Solution Effect Analysis tests a potential course of action and identifies its effects. It will help you to:

❑ see whether the decision you intend to make actually solves the problem you want to solve;
❑ compare the effects of different alternatives;
❑ check that a solution does not cause other problems;
❑ identify the actions you will need to take to ensure successful implementation.

1. *Define the course of action you are assessing.*
2. *Identify the major categories* within which you want to assess effects of the solution. As with selection criteria, choice of categories is critically important in ensuring that the effects of a decision are properly assessed.
3. *Explore the potential effects of the decision within each category.* Take time over this: allow your mind to 'work out' the effects within an area. If one category becomes overloaded, a key area of the course of action may need further investigation.
4. *Analyse the effects.* Highlight any effects that need immediate action, and linkages between effects. Look out for unexpected effects – and effects of effects. Above all, don't ignore any adverse effects or new problems. You may need to balance the difficulties you anticipate against the benefits of implementing the decision.

A diagram will help you to follow the progress of your analysis more clearly. Draw it in exactly the same way as a fishbone diagram, placing the solution on the left side of a page and drawing a horizontal line from it, adding a stem at 45° for each major category. Add further stems for the potential effects within each category.

CASE STUDY

Tom works for a large national clearing bank. He has been given the task of finding a solution to the bank's growing mountain of client files: 35,000 are currently in storage; two million pieces of paper are being added every year. New regulations demand that records are kept longer, in more secure ways, and with a retrieval time for any document of 48 hours. Legal requirements mean that any document held by the bank must be acceptable in a court of law.

He considers that he has three options. He could maintain records on paper and find better or cheaper storage facilities; he could transfer all records to microfilm with computer-aided retrieval; and he could store the records electronically, on CD-ROM.

This is a technical decision, subject to a large number of measurable variables. The costs of each option need to be estimated: transfer costs, projected operating costs, and comparisons between the two. Tom will have to take into account the rental of storage space (in various locations, in different styles of warehousing and with different types of lease), equipment costs (and the prospects for technological development) and personnel costs. Retrieval issues, including the number of documents to be retrieved regularly, travel between sites, deterioration of paper, access to microfilm and electronic networking must be considered. There are also security implications with each option: the physical security of warehousing, the possibility of theft, the dangers of tampering with an electronic record.

Tom's task is a complex one. However, the number of options before him is small. He is in danger of being overwhelmed by complexity, of measuring everything. Clear objectives and requirements of any proposed system will help him to concentrate on the most important issues. Does the bank want a system that is cheap to install or cheap to maintain? Does it want a system that creates easy access for large numbers of people? Does it envisage business growing or changing in the future in any way that would affect its need to retrieve documents: product development, customer profiling?

Continued on next page

Continued from previous page

Ranking and Rating will certainly help him to make his decision: some requirements of any proposed storage system are essential (regulatory and legal requirements, for example), others are desirable. The consequences of each option can be mapped out in financial, technical, administrative and personnel terms using Solution Effect Analysis; and a careful cost/benefit analysis will allow Tom to make his final choice, making an overall assessment of the probability of success and the balance of risk against reward – an essential factor when Tom presents his preferred solution to the managers who will approve the decision.

Other people's views

A decision will involve other people. We will need to estimate the consequences of our decision, to both those who implement it and anybody whose work will change because of it: system users, other managers, other departments, customers, regulators, the press, the public....

Decisions can be fundamentally influenced by other people's views. Nicholas Nicholaidis, in the late 1950s, investigated decisions made by 332 public sector officials in the US. He discovered that, far from being rationally worked out, most decisions in such bureaucratic cultures were coloured by emotion, power politics, personal influence and the decision maker's own values. Many decisions were made on the basis of dangerously incomplete information and without considering all of the available options. Decision makers tended to settle, not for the best or optimum solution, but for the course of action that:

- ❏ agreed as much as possible with their own interests and values;
- ❏ agreed with the values of their line managers;
- ❏ were acceptable to those implementing the decision and those affected by it;
- ❏ appeared to be 'reasonable' in its context;
- ❏ had a justification or excuse 'built in', in case the decision had unexpected consequences.

Nearly every decision maker consulted or involved others and their decisions were usually compromises that pleased as many people as possible.

Experience suggests that decisions are still being made like this in many organizations. Perhaps the problem is not that other people's views are being considered, but that managers are tending to consider them in the wrong way.

A decision will depend for its effectiveness on other people. We must take their views into account; but we must also be careful not to compromise our own objectives, or the interests of the organization as a whole, for the sake of 'an easy ride'. Decision making, like politics, is the art of the possible.

When considering the possible consequences of your decision on other people, ask:

❏ Who would be affected – now and in the future? Short and long term?
❏ How will they be affected?
❏ What are/will be their views?
❏ What effect could those views have on the success of our decision?
❏ How could we address those views?
❏ Can we prioritize some people for attention?

Answering these questions will lead you towards Force Field Analysis and all the associated issues of communicating your decision that we address in Chapter 5.

Making a final choice

If you still have to make a choice, it should now be between two clear options. You are facing an *either ... or*.

Alternatives, strictly speaking, are mutually exclusive. You may have chosen them because they both score equally, because they are attractive, or because they are the two 'least worst' options.

Maybe you could choose both; or combine them in some way. You could, of course, decide to do nothing. If neither alternative appeals to you, and compromise or mixing is not possible, a conscious decision not to act may be worth considering.

You might also decide on the option that best keeps your future options open. All decisions are provisional. Maybe the best decision at this stage is to do whatever is necessary to accommodate future change and leave yourself ready for another decision later.

Making the final choice may involve asking these questions:

❑ Which of your possible options are feasible, given your current:
  – authority;
  – resources;
  – abilities?
❑ Which of the feasible options give the best objective chances of success (appraisal against criteria: assessment of consequences)?
❑ Are the final options true alternatives? Could you do:
  – both (simultaneously or in sequence)?
  – a combination of the two?
❑ Is a compromise solution feasible or attractive?
❑ Would it be better to do nothing?
❑ Which option would help you keep your options open for as long as possible? When and why should you decide not to keep your options open?

At last, we have reached the final choice: whether to proceed with a single course of action, or not. With luck, we have chosen the best option – given current circumstances and intelligent estimates of probability. Now we must commit to it: and, as we shall see, there is an enormous difference between choosing a course of action and taking it.

EVALUATING A DECISION

❏ Is it simple? Does it seem obvious? Is it too complicated?
❏ Is it exciting? Will it 'explode' in people's minds?
❏ Is it reasonable? Would most people accept it as sensible?
❏ Is it easy to explain? Can you summarize it in a single sentence?
❏ Is it timely? Why pursue it now? Would it be better to wait? Can you afford to wait?

And what if, after all this work, we still have not made a choice? We have not failed. Remember that thinking towards decisions is a design process. Nothing has been wasted: indeed, we may have saved a great deal of time and money by rejecting a potentially disastrous decision.

When we are designing solutions, 'back to the drawing board' is not the cry of ignominious defeat. Complete the decision cycle by going back to Step 1 and reviewing your objectives and the problem you want to solve. The very best decision we can make will only be the best at the time.

3

CONSULTING

Very few decisions will be made in isolation. Even if we take the decision alone, making it happen will almost certainly involve others.

Experience suggests that group decision making is usually not practical or effective. Yet, if people are not involved in the decisions that affect them, gaining their commitment will be difficult. And with the increasing emphasis on empowerment and devolving decisions to those best fitted to make them, consultation has become a critical factor in the process.

Consultation here refers to thinking with others towards a decision. Consulting after the decision has been made is little more than a pretence and can cause justifiable resentment.

CONSULT OR PARTICIPATE?

We consult in order to:

❑ clarify ownership of the decision;
❑ clarify the reason for the decision with those consulted;
❑ check others' points of view;
❑ use the expertise of others;
❑ gain commitment to the decision from those affected by it;
❑ enrich our own thinking by using others' thinking skills;
❑ test our thinking with others.

It is important to distinguish consultation from participation. A manager who consults prior to making a decision retains responsibility for the decision and its consequences. Inviting others to participate in the decision making process implies that all the participants will share some or all of the responsibility.

STYLES OF DECISION MAKING

Robert Tannenbaum and Warren Schmidt identified seven broad styles of decision making in management, which they placed on a 'continuum of leadership behaviour'. They visualized a decision as being like a cake that could be divided up in different ways between manager and team.

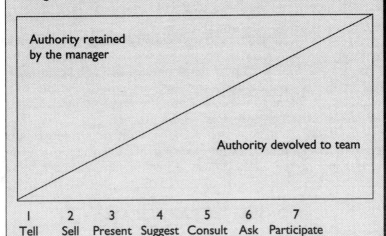

Authority retained by the manager

Authority devolved to team

1	2	3	4	5	6	7
Tell	Sell	Present	Suggest	Consult	Ask	Participate

1. **Tell.** The manager makes the decision single-handed, with little or no attempt to involve others or ask their opinions in advance.
2. **Sell.** The manager makes the decision and presents it as a proposal to those affected by it, so that they can express their opinions. 'Selling' the idea, like selling a product, involves negotiation, identifying needs, promoting the benefits of the idea to the 'customers', and being willing to accept the prospect of a 'failed sale'. Responsibility for the decision remains firmly with the individual manager.

Continued on next page

Continued from previous page

3. **Present.** The manager presents some of the background to the decision and invites questions so that the team can explore and understand it.
4. **Suggest.** The manager suggests a possible course of action, invites discussion and review by the team, but reserves the right to make the final decision.
5. **Consult.** The manager consults those affected in advance, making it clear that no decision has yet been made but that responsibility rests with the manager alone. Others may offer their views and suggestions, and may be involved in the decision cycle. The manager promises to consider everybody's views carefully but reserves the right to make the decision alone.
6. **Ask.** At this point, the team has responsibility for the decision. The manager defines the choice and the limits or parameters of the discussion.
7. **Participate.** A joint decision is arrived at with full involvement by everybody affected. The manager's views carry no more weight than those of anybody else. The decision is made by consensus or by voting. The manager agrees to support the majority decision, even if not agreeing with it.

As empowerment becomes the watchword of managerial best practice and teamwork grows ever more common, there is perhaps an increasing fashion to regard the 'telling' style as 'bad' and 'participative management' as self-evidently 'good'. In reality, different styles of decision making will depend on the nature of the decision to be made. Telling may be the only option available if the decision involves:

❏ hiring and firing;
❏ confidentiality;
❏ health and safety;
❏ critical urgency.

Your own style will be affected by the nature of the decision, the relationship you have with your team and the overall culture or style of the organization. Perhaps the most important advice must be to maintain a certain consistency in your managerial decision making. Inviting your team to join in making decisions one minute, only to overrule them with an order the next, will only create resentment, confusion and unhappiness.

I will continue in this chapter to refer to 'consultation': the process of asking others for their advice, opinions, expert knowledge or experience in order to enrich our own thinking. Most of what I say will be applicable, too, in participative or team decision making.

THE DANGERS OF CONSULTING

Consulting prior to a decision is so obviously useful that it can be easy to ignore the dangers associated with it.

Lack of authenticity
Consulting 'for the look of it' can be worse than not consulting at all. It will breed resentment, bad feeling and suspicion in your team – and with good reason. If you only seem to consult but have actually made up your mind, you are behaving dishonestly.

Loss of control
Consultation implies that you, the manager, are still responsible for the decision. Allowing others to participate in the decision shifts the responsibility. You – and your team – need to know exactly who 'carries the can'.

Plummeting morale
Making it known that you are considering a certain decision can have an adverse effect on your team's morale. You will need to be prepared for that.

Rumour
Similarly, a consultation period can be rife with rumour, and with stories of doom and gloom. It may be difficult to be entirely open and retain confidentiality. Be as honest as you can, about the issues and about ownership of the decision.

Confusion

Your team may not be used to having their opinions canvassed. They may not be sure what you require of them. Be ready to make your needs clear.

Confrontation

Any difficult decision will produce resistance; some will generate 'politics'. As well as making it clear what you want your team to do, you will need to guide them through the thinking process that will result in the decision. Follow the decision cycle and make sure that the team knows how it works. Your overall aim in consulting is to involve others in making the decision. Involvement in the decision will foster commitment to its implementation.

> *People don't resist change. They resist being changed.*
> quoted by Peter Senge

WHOM TO CONSULT

Consult whoever will enrich your thinking about the issue. You will want to consult others on the basis of their:

❏ expertise;
❏ experience;
❏ authority to support any decision you make.

Whom you consult will obviously depend on the nature of the decision you must make. For expertise you might go to:

❏ your team;
❏ individuals with specific skills or knowledge areas;
❏ users of systems or procedures;
❏ suppliers of products or services;
❏ independent advisers or consultants.

For experience, search out any of the above as well as:

❏ customers;
❏ a mentor;

❏ colleagues;
❏ senior managers.

Professional consultants can be enormously useful in delivering new expertise. What they cannot do is deliver the unique and priceless experience of your colleagues within the organization. This awareness of the balance between experience and expertise, and of those who can help you in these areas, will be invaluable to you in the consultation process.

> *Ask the man who does the job.*
> W Edwards Deming

And for authority, you will need to seek allies who can give your idea support; 'spheres of influence' who can wield power in the organization on your behalf:

❏ senior managers;
❏ budget holders;
❏ heads of departments;
❏ technical, financial or legal managers.

CONSULTATION BY CONVERSATION

The basic unit of consultation is the conversation. Whether with another individual or in a group, in person or on paper, conversation is the means by which we will explore others' views.

A well-managed conversation will begin with both, or all, participants being clear about the conversation's objectives. The aim of a consultative conversation is to develop the decision maker's thinking; the aim of a participative conversation is to work towards agreement about a course of action.

FOUR TYPES OF CONVERSATION

Michael Wallaczek identifies four broad types of conversation.

❑ *A conversation for relationship*
An exploration. Who are we? What links us? How can we understand each other? Where do we stand? Can we stand together? What do you see that I can't see? What do I see that you don't see? Meeting somebody socially for the first time, or the early part of a job interview, are good examples.

❑ *A conversation for possibility*
Nurturing an idea at an early stage. Exploring alternatives. Not going as far as seeking options or planning. A delicate conversation: inappropriate jokes, judgemental comments or 'explosions' are not allowed. Brainstorming is a good example.

❑ *A conversation for opportunity*
Formulating rough plans. Sifting the feasible from the possible. Assessing available resources, support and skills for a project. The bridge from possibility to opportunity is measurement or conditions of satisfaction. The final part of an appraisal might be a good example.

❑ *A conversation for action*
A dynamic between requesting and promising. Offers and counteroffers are made; conditions of satisfaction are spelled out; timescales and plans are made clear. Delegating a task is a good example.

Know which kind of conversation you are holding. Make the conversation's purpose explicit: follow the guidelines for each.

Keep the conversation on track by having a plan.

1. Identify the issues to be discussed and enrich your thinking about them.
2. Generate alternatives and explore them.
3. Draw conclusions and identify material that you can usefully take forward.

Try to keep to your plan. If ideas emerge or concerns are raised at the 'wrong' point in the conversation, note them down and return to them at the appropriate moment.

Adversarial thinking

Much is made in management theory of the virtue of conflict in conversation. It is said that debate between people with differing views is not merely unavoidable in business, but essential; that discussions around important decisions cannot be cool and calm but must inevitably involve heated argument. A recent article in *Harvard Business Review* calls this process 'creative abrasion'.

Many senior managers persist in regarding conflict as fundamental to group thinking. 'Business is conflict', cries Richard Snyder, formerly head of Simon & Schuster. 'That's the creative process. You don't get excellence by saying yes.'

> *The understanding that underlies the right decision grows out of the clash and conflict of divergent opinions and out of the serious consideration of competing alternatives.*
>
> Peter Drucker

I find this hard to take. The 'serious consideration of competing alternatives' will surely be hampered by 'the clash and conflict of divergent opinions'.

Opinions are ideas gone cold. They are our generalized assumptions about what might be true – or what should be true – rather than what is true in specific circumstances. Stories, explanations, justifications, excuses, gossip, criticism: all are forms of opinion. They are the enemies of good thinking. (Interestingly, Snyder himself apparently gained a reputation for vulgarity and violent personal attacks in his strategy meetings.)

'Debate' is merely the polite name for argument based on opinions. It is the most formal forum for 'adversarial thinking', the curse of conversations everywhere. Edward de Bono has coined this phrase to describe thinking that searches for the truth by arguing from fixed positions: a kind of intellectual boxing match, in which we seek to batter our opponent into submission (the word 'debate' means 'to beat down').

We accord such thinking enormous prestige. It is at the heart of the Western intellectual tradition and is, to some extent, the basis of the scientific method. It forms the structure of our legal procedure (prosecution and defence) and our political system (government and opposition). It is the commonest method by which journalism and the media investigate issues – mainly because watching a good row is entertaining. It is such a powerful model of thinking that most of us regard it as the only kind of organized thinking.

Adversarial thinking usually appears in one of three forms.

❑ *Ego thinking*

We become identified with our ideas. Criticism of an idea quickly becomes an attack on the person holding it. The 'serious consideration of competing alternatives' becomes the use of debate to score points against others. Logic (which can be used to support virtually any proposition) is used to bolster emotion; opinion carries the same weight as evidence.

❑ *Rigid thinking*

Adversarial thinking starts from propositions about reality rather than an exploration of reality. It is limited to an examination of those propositions: any thinking that strays beyond their boundaries can be dismissed as 'irrelevant'. Indeed, the adversarial mode actually serves to entrench propositions rather than adapt or modify them.

❑ *Political thinking*

Because ideas become identified with individuals, people realize that achieving action is a matter of aligning themselves with ideas, and with those promoting them. Because rigid thinking limits the growth of ideas, propositions can only be attacked or defended. A great deal of energy is devoted to creating 'power bases' and undermining 'opponents', to bureaucratic conniving, behind-the-scenes manipulation and rumour-mongering.

As managers of conversations, we must be continually on the alert for these three dangerous varieties of adversarial thinking.

Balancing advocacy and enquiry

All conversation is founded on a dynamic of speaking and listening: telling and asking, the balance of advocacy and enquiry. The success of any conversation depends on how that dynamic is managed.

We tend to be much better at advocacy than enquiry. Most managers have been well trained in the techniques of presenting, arguing and explaining a case. We are often less skilled in asking questions, investigating and exploring an issue, or examining the assumptions that lie behind our view of it. Debate, of course, involves no asking whatever: we listen only for the flaws in opponents' argument that will allow us to attack them.

This imbalance is reinforced by organizational cultures that value certainty and the ability to stand your ground. Where 'decisiveness' is rewarded, ego thinking, rigid thinking and political thinking are likely to flourish.

These trends are changing, partly because 'macho' management itself is becoming less tolerated. If we wish to enrich our thinking and improve the quality of our decisions, we must learn to redress the balance. We must become more skilled in enquiry.

THE LADDER OF INFERENCE

Chris Argyris has created a powerful model for understanding and influencing our conversations.

Argyris pictures thinking as a ladder. At the bottom of the ladder is observation; at the top is action. Making a decision is essentially a matter of climbing the ladder.

❑ From our *observation*, we select data and step on to the first rung.
❑ On the second rung, we add *meaning* from our experience of similar data.
❑ On the third, we generalize those meanings into *assumptions*.
❑ On the fourth, we construct mental models or *beliefs* out of those assumptions. We view the world through these mental models.

Our beliefs dictate our actions.

Continued on next page

Continued from previous page

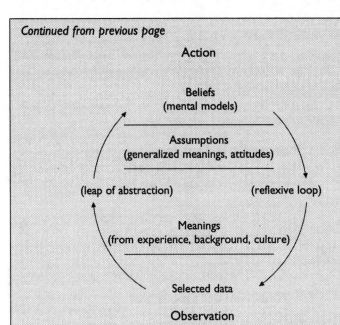

Action

Beliefs
(mental models)

Assumptions
(generalized meanings, attitudes)

(leap of abstraction)   (reflexive loop)

Meanings
(from experience, background, culture)

Selected data

Observation

A conversation is a journey up and down the ladder. We are so good at climbing it that we can leap all the rungs in a matter of seconds in a 'leap of abstraction', substituting assumptions for observation and belief for meaning. Indeed, our beliefs will help us to jump down the ladder by dictating what data to select in future (a 'reflexive loop').

The trick is to be able to stand still on a rung of the ladder. We can use the ladder to:

❏ make our thinking more visible to others;
❏ ask others about their thinking;
❏ offer our own thinking for enquiry.

The last objective is an important one. Others may initially be surprised at our willingness to renounce ownership of an idea. By making our intentions clear, however, and inviting others to examine our own thinking, we can encourage them to make their own contributions more willingly.

Continued on next page

Continued from previous page

Using these interventions requires no special training or awareness on anybody else's part. They can have an immediate and dramatic effect on the quality of our conversations.

There are plenty of remarks that we can use on each rung of the ladder. Here are a few to point the way.

Making our thinking more visible to others

Action	This is what I think we should do.
Belief	I think that, in general....
Assumption	I'm assuming here that....
Meaning	Let me tell you why I see it like this.
Selected data	This is what I've chosen to look at.
Observation	I've been looking at this area.

Asking others about their thinking

Action	What makes this a good plan?
Belief	Can you take me through your thinking?
Assumption	Do you think you might be assuming that...?
Meaning	Does this mean that you think...?
Selected data	What led you to look at this in particular?
Observation	Where have you been looking around?

Offering our own thinking for enquiry

Action	Can you see why we shouldn't do this?
Belief	Do you see things differently?
Assumption	Are my assumptions valid?
Meaning	Would you see a different meaning for this result?
Selected data	What have I missed?
Observation	Am I looking in the wrong place?

Increasing the range of our thinking

Serious conversations should seek to distinguish ideas from people. Edward de Bono's 'Six Thinking Hats' are becoming increasingly popular as tools for helping to make these distinctions clear.

De Bono suggests that every contribution to a conversation is labelled by means of a coloured 'hat' that the speaker is 'wearing' as they make it. This helps us to register for ourselves and for others the nature of the remark and its function in the conversation. Leaders of conversations can also ask contributors deliberately to make contributions 'wearing' a particular hat.

❑ White hat: facts and figures.
❑ Red hat: emotion, feelings, hunches and intuition.
❑ Black hat: caution, judgement, fitting propositions to facts.
❑ Yellow hat: advantages, benefits, savings.
❑ Green hat: creativity, new ideas, exploration, suggestions.
❑ Blue hat: thinking about thinking, control of the thinking process, 'points of order'.

The great beauty of de Bono's hats is that we can put them on and take them off very easily. It would be utterly inappropriate to suggest that someone is a 'red-hat thinker' or a 'black-hat thinker'. Anybody can use the hats whenever they want. Indeed, using the hats allows people to make remarks that they might not ordinarily risk making. The hats serve to objectify the thinking process – and to make everybody think in different ways.

APPOINTING A CONSULTATIVE TEAM

You may be able to gather together a team to engage in consultation. Many project teams are formed specifically to research an issue and recommend a decision. Increasing numbers of organizations use project teams, formed specifically to research an area, recommend a decision and even implement it.

Appointing a team can have a number of advantages.

❑ Teams are better at gathering and analysing information than individuals.
❑ Teams can pool expertise and create a focus on particular objectives.
❑ Teamwork can generate new ideas and alternatives more quickly.

❑ Assumptions, prejudice and bias can be countered by team-work.
❑ Giving a team ownership of a decision can generate commitment to implementation.

Decision making in teams, however, can also be fraught with difficulties.

❑ *Blurred responsibility*
Project teams are all too often appointed with unclear objectives and, worse still, unclear authority. The distinction between consultation and participation is critically important in setting up the team. Who does the team report to? What is the authority and responsibility of the team leader? Who will make the decision?
❑ *Groupthink*
Putting a group of people together and assuming that they will think well as a group is risky. There is no guarantee that calling a group of people a 'team' will prevent ego thinking, rigid thinking or political thinking. In the absence of properly managed thinking, the team's instinct to survive may result in groupthink: thinking limited to the conventions by which the group maintains its identity. Awkward questions, disagreements, divergent perspectives and uncomfortable information can be suppressed by the group – or repressed by group members before they even utter them.
❑ *Status*
Working in a team will not necessarily iron out perceived differences in authority. People with higher status may be dangerously influential in manipulating ideas and information.
❑ *Expertise*
Appointing people on the basis of their expertise can also prove dangerous. Experts may concentrate on their specialist areas, ignoring areas they know little about. Simply putting experts from different disciplines together into a 'multi-functional' team does not assure good thinking. They may not be able even to talk a common language.

Follow these principles in appointing any team to think as a group.

❏ *Clarify the team's objectives*
  Make it clear why the team is being formed, what they are expected to produce, to whom they report and what the timescale is.
❏ *Clarify the thinking process*
  Make sure that everybody on the team understands the decision cycle and how to operate it. Make sure also that the team uses it. Develop the team's conversational skills.
❏ *Clarify responsibilities*
  Specify the role of the team and of each team member. Allocate explicit action responsibilities and monitor individuals' progress against each. In particular, make sure that the team leader is clear about their responsibilities and accountability.
❏ *Motivate and encourage the team in their work*
  Do not use the appointment of the team as an excuse to 'shift the monkey', to abnegate your own responsibility for the decision. Too many project teams founder because they are left to operate in a vacuum.

Running team meetings

Consultative teams must meet frequently. The danger for any regular meeting is that it can collapse into a routine: soon it comes to be regarded more with dread than interest.

The solution might be to change the way the meetings are run. A team leader who is willing to delegate functions to other team members will lead meetings that are more active, more involving and more successful.

Remember: the aim of any regular meeting must be to keep it as short as possible.

How to do it:

❏ *The team leader constructs the agenda informally prior to the meeting*
  Anyone who wants to contribute sends a note or adds it to the list. E-mail is particularly valuable for this.

❑ *The agenda is finalized at the start of the meeting*
Each participant must justify the inclusion of their item on the agenda. The meeting decides whether it is worthy of discussion: perhaps another team member can solve the problem outside the meeting: a brief conversation, a memo, a report put in the internal post.

❑ *All items decided on for the agenda are given timings*
The whole meeting has a maximum length – decided upon by the team leader – which it must not exceed. The aim is not to fill the allotted time, but to complete the meeting as quickly as possible.

❑ *Nothing else is allowed until the next meeting*

❑ *Each item is 'owned' by the participant who submitted it*
They become the Chair for that item. As discussion progresses, they must ask:
  – Is the task or problem clearly understood?
  – Is expertise identified?
  – Is knowledge shared?
  – Are they creating a co-operative climate in the group?
  – Is everyone being heard?
  – Can a decision be reached by consensus – without a vote?
  – Is the Chair's role reduced to a minimum?

❑ *The Chair for each item becomes the minute-taker for the next item,* recording the minutes on a flip chart for all to see.

❑ *Timings are strictly adhered to*
The responsibility of each Chair.

❑ *At the end of the meeting, decisions and actions are summarized by the team leader,* who then invites any initial suggestions for the next meeting.

The result of this procedure is increased ownership of the meeting by the whole team. A climate of openness allows all views to be expressed with equal authority; solutions are arrived at by agreement rather than imposed. Adopting this procedure may cut the amount of time the team spends meeting by a third.

Brainstorming

Brainstorming is the most famous technique for generating ideas in teams. It was developed in the early 1950s by Alex Osborn, an advertising agency executive. Osborn was apparently inspired by a technique that had been used by Hindu teachers in India for more than 400 years. The Indian name for the technique is *Prai-Barshana*, meaning 'questioning outside yourself'. Brainstorming, like *Prai-Barshana*, seeks to generate ideas without becoming possessive, critical, analytical or evaluative.

The basic principles of brainstorming are that: all judgemental thinking is suspended; 'freewheeling' – associative thinking, wild ideas – is welcome; the more ideas the better (quantity not quality!); and combining ideas, or improving on them, is to be encouraged.

Any brainstorming session should abide by a few simple rules.

❑ Keep it short – 30 minutes is ideal – with a strict time limit.
❑ Not too many participants: 6–12.
❑ Include as wide a range of people as possible.
❑ Seats are best in a semi-circle with no tables: Chair sitting anywhere; Administrator standing at a flip chart.
❑ The Chair must:
  – define, but not analyse, the problem at the start of the session;
  – stop everyone talking at once;
  – make sure quieter participants contribute;
  – prevent evaluation of ideas;
  – redefine the problem at various points in the meeting;
  – check that the Administrator has every idea;
  – be ready with ideas when the flow stops;
  – ask for a review of ideas when the flow dries up;
  – bring the session to a close.
❑ The Administrator must:
  – note down every idea contributed;
  – condense them for inclusion on the list;
  – check with participants on the meaning;
  – demand a pause if they cannot keep up;

- never refuse to list an idea, even if they feel it repeats an earlier one;
- not contribute any ideas of their own.
❑ No analysis of the problem is allowed.
❑ No evaluation of ideas is allowed: on the basis of relevance, quality of idea, practicality, common sense or anything else.

An experienced group can generate up to 200 ideas in 30 minutes. These are analysed, later, in an evaluation session:

❑ List the obviously useful ideas.
❑ Dismiss ideas which have already been tried and failed.
❑ Note ideas which can be tried easily, immediately – and cheaply.
❑ Note promising ideas.
❑ List ideas needing further thought or research.
❑ Extract useful aspects from silly ideas. These may produce new ideas.

The result should be new lists of:

❑ ideas for immediate trial;
❑ ideas for further exploration.

4

COMMITTING

Committing is at the very heart of decision making. A decision, as we defined it earlier, is a commitment to action. There is a great difference between choosing to do something and committing yourself to do it.

Committing is the act of:

❑ deciding your responsibility: what action you will take;
❑ using your authority to make it happen; and
❑ making yourself accountable for the consequences.

No wonder that commitment is, for many managers, sometimes the most uncomfortable part of the process.

Faced with a difficult decision, some managers feel tempted to ask their team to commit to it collectively. Such commitment, however, is unlikely to be successful.

❑ If a team has to take collective responsibility for a decision, groupthink may make it opt for consensus or compromise, particularly when the decision is complicated or controversial. The result may be a lack of clear direction and ineffective action, for which few people will feel any enthusiasm.

Paradoxically, groupthink can also result in highly risky decisions. A team may feel it can act more dangerously if everyone takes collective responsibility; indeed, it may choose a dangerous course of action precisely in order to strengthen its own identity.

Teams become especially vulnerable to both compromise and high-risk decisions if governed by strong or rigid values: a sense of overweening competitiveness or gung-ho adventurism, blind adherence to ideology or an obligation to be 'politically correct'.

❑ Authority, too – the power or right to make the decision happen – can be dangerously skewed when it is shared by a group of people. At best, majorities will tend to outvote minorities and make no provision for the needs of the latter; at worst, authority can be hijacked by one or a few powerful people and threaten team identity.

❑ Team accountability all too often means no accountability at all. The 'buck stops nowhere': if questions or problems arise, nobody is available to sort them out.

Commitment, then, rests best with one person. Teams may be very useful as consultants during the decision cycle: identifying problems, generating alternatives, analysing information, sifting options. The final choice may be the 'least worst' option; it may be a very finely balanced choice. Many business decisions have some disadvantages and very few are likely to please everybody. Some decisions demand courage and the resolution to face unpopularity. After all, it is part of your responsibility as a manager to make such decisions.

What difficulties, then, do we face in finding this commitment?

❑ *Lack of time*
It can be hard to feel committed to a decision made hurriedly or under pressure – particularly when we know or suspect that it will be overtaken or contradicted by another in the near future. We may be recklessly keen to 'get on and do something' and give ourselves no time to think.

❑ *Lack of consultation*
We feel inadequately briefed or prepared; that we are leaping in the dark; that we cannot foresee the consequences clearly. We may have failed to listen to others' views, opinions and suggestions adequately, or failed to assemble sufficient information.

❑ *Too much of both!*
We have too much time to worry, to ponder the alternatives and consequences. We have consulted so much, and have so much information in front of us, that we have lost sight of the important issue under a mountain of detail.

❑ *Fudge*
It can be hard to feel committed to a decision that is designed to please everybody but will satisfy nobody.

❑ *Lack of support*
You may be working in an organization that is 'risk-averse'; or, alternatively, that encourages you to be 'trigger-happy' and make snap decisions without careful thought.

❑ *Lack of emotional commitment*
Commitment is not merely the rational agreement that a decision is a good one. It is also the belief, the emotional energy and enthusiasm for a decision that will help you to motivate yourself and others. We may, in the end, be simply frightened of taking the first step.

Committing to a decision is committing to a *risk*. Risk can be managed by identifying two dimensions: *objective risk* and *emotional risk*.

MANAGING OBJECTIVE RISK

We have seen that it is possible to quantify risk, using two calculations:

❑ the probability of success;
❑ the balance of risk and reward.

If these calculations do not deliver wholehearted commitment, it is perhaps because we are concerned about the probability and cost of failure. Managing objective risk is a matter of:

❑ identifying the reasons for the risk of failure;
❑ making contingency plans.

We must identify potential problems, assess their seriousness, rank them in order and make plans to deal with each.

FAILURE PREVENTION ANALYSIS

Failure Prevention Analysis (FPA) is a systematic technique for estimating what could go wrong with a decision. Identifying possible failures, we can plan actions that remove or reduce the chance of these failures occurring.

Use FPA when your decision may result in unclear action responsibilities, when failure could have major or catastrophic consequences, when many teams, departments or people are involved, or when there are few alternatives to your proposed decisions.

FPA involves four steps.

1. *Identify vulnerable areas of implementation and potential failures.* Have a clear idea of your implementation plan: the methods, arrangements and features of the action you propose. Ask: 'What could go wrong?' Consulting and brainstorming could be useful here.
2. *Rank each potential failure by noting its consequences.* Estimate:
   - the probability of the failure occurring;
   - the seriousness of the consequences.
   Rate both probability and seriousness on a scale of ten. Multiply both ratings to give an overall rating for each potential failure.

Possible failure	Probability (max: 10)	Consequence (max: 10)	Overall rating
A	8	1	8
B	3	10	30
C	9	5	45
D	2	0	0
E	4	5	20

It can be useful to evaluate possible failures according to two distinct criteria:
- consequences for customers;
- consequences for the organization.

Continued on next page

> *Continued from previous page*
>
> 3. ***Examine causes of key potential failures.*** Use fishbone dia-grams or systems thinking to help you. Look for root causes rather than intermediate causes or symptoms.
> 4. ***Identify preventive actions.*** Such actions should aim to eliminate or reduce the root cause of potential failure. They will only reduce the risk of failure: they may not be able to guarantee prevention of failure. Such preventive measures, however, will help to tip the scales in favour of success.

Making plans for implementing the decision will also help us to feel that it is truly feasible.

❑ Review the objectives of the planned action.
❑ Rank them according to importance. What *must* we achieve? What would we like to achieve?
❑ Set targets and deadlines.
❑ Establish 'milestones' along the way to measure progress against your objectives.
❑ Allocate responsibility for specific actions.
❑ Plan the process of co-ordination between action holders.

MANAGING EMOTIONAL RISK

All the work we have outlined in this book will help you to prepare to commit to a decision. Rational decision making, though, ignores one critical factor: our emotional commitment to risk. How can we manage that?

The moment of commitment is a 'point of no return': the moment when we leap from the diving board and commit to flying towards the water. It involves courage, no matter how much preparation, testing and calculating we have done.

In every success story, you find someone has made a courageous decision.
Peter Drucker

Finding that courage may be difficult. Without it, we find a number of ways of deferring commitment.

❑ *Rabbit in the headlights*
We are paralysed with indecision and wait for fate to strike.
❑ *Head in the sand*
Ignore the problem and maybe it will go away. Sometimes, of course, it does! More likely, it will develop, grow and change shape.
❑ *Jump first, ask questions later*
A high-risk option, chosen by many a manager in distress.
❑ *Consult an oracle*
Oracles are useful if we are seeking truth, but hopeless if we want to know what to do. Consulting an oracle, as we have seen, is an interesting creative technique for provoking new ideas; it will not, however, let us see into the future. Oracles can be addictive, too, fuelling superstition and paranoia. Many leaders, from Julius Caesar to Ronald Reagan, are said to have used oracles and astrologers to help them make important decisions. You have been warned.

Are there any more better ways to manage the emotional risk of committing to a decision?

CASE STUDY

John has just become purchasing manager for a toy manufacturer. He is facing a tough decision.

The company has been supplied for many years by Reid Mouldings, a small, family-run firm producing plastic parts. Over the years, John's company has become Reid's sole customer.

The quality of the mouldings has been good; there have never been any production or delivery difficulties. But Reid has not moved with the times: they have failed to invest in new equipment and they remain overstaffed. John's predecessor has managed to justify using Reid's in the face of increasingly obvious competition, out of loyalty to a local firm in an area of high unemployment.

Continued on next page

Continued from previous page

John is faced with a target to cut costs by 10 per cent in his first year. He knows that he can purchase cheaper mouldings, of higher quality, from a firm in Italy: he has made enquiries and received costings; a contract is ready to be signed. He needs only to commit to his decision – and terminate his contract with Reid Mouldings.

His decision will probably cost the jobs of 30 people. He understands that the business decision is an obvious one; he appreciates that he cannot take responsibility for Reid's own management decisions; he knows that his firm will not have to pay unemployment benefit to thirty people. None of this makes the decision any easier emotionally.

He writes a letter to Reid's MD, terminating the contract. His manager understands his position and praises him for making such a difficult decision so early in his post. But John does not sleep that night.

Recognizing your fears

What are you afraid of? Maybe you are anxious about:

❑ things going wrong;
❑ others' responses;
❑ feeling out of control;
❑ feeling inadequate – 'not up to the job'.

What, objectively, is the worst that could go wrong? Stare the possibility in the face. What would be the consequences of this worst case scenario? What would be the consequences of not making the decision?

We may feel under considerable pressure to 'get it right'. Thinking, in such circumstances, may make things worse; over-reliance on the tools of rational decision making can serve only to increase our anxiety. The only answer may be to make a move and see what happens. You will not know whether you have got it right until you try. Plan as much as you can; try to be ready for what you have not foreseen.

What might other people think about the decision – and about you? What is the worst they could think – or do? How likely is that? Remember: people are likely to respect you for making a clear decision, for being open and honest.

Robert Fritz claims that all of us are prey to two deep-seated beliefs that inhibit our ability to meet challenges:

❏ a sense of powerlessness: that we lack the ability to achieve what we want;
❏ a sense of unworthiness: that, in some way, we do not deserve to succeed.

These beliefs can take possession of us very easily. They can manifest themselves in different ways: a loss of energy or enthusiasm; an inability to finish tasks; 'treadmill thinking' or uselessly repetitive behaviour; unexpected obstacles; the sense that people are letting us down.

We can use a variety of 'coping strategies' for dealing with such deep-seated beliefs.

❏ *Eroding the vision*
We chip away at our objectives and convince ourselves that we would be satisfied with lesser achievements.
❏ *Conflict manipulation*
We focus on what we do not want rather than what we want; we become 'anti' in our attitudes and concentrate on the forces ranged against us. Maybe we try to motivate ourselves and others by talking more about the consequences of failure than the prospects of success.
❏ *Willpower*
We 'psych' ourselves up and focus obsessively on targets, on getting the job done, to the detriment of anything else. We are willing to 'pay any price'; we are ready to defeat any opposition.

None of these strategies addresses the deep beliefs of powerlessness or unworthiness themselves. They may tackle the symptoms but they will not remove the underlying cause.

It is important to recognize such behavioural patterns when they occur. Watch out for 'early warning' signs and ask whether some deep belief might be governing your actions.

Be kind to yourself. A belief, once recognized, can be altered. By recognizing the demon, you have registered a part of yourself that is not prey to it: you become no longer possessed by it. Ask what you need to do to change your behaviour; and how you may be able to change the underlying belief.

If you recognize a 'coping strategy' at work, ask:

❏ What am I doing right now? What am I thinking? What am I feeling?
❏ What do I want right now? What am I trying to achieve? What decision am I trying to make? What am I trying to avoid? What do I really want?
❏ What am I doing right now to prevent me getting what I want? What is blocking my path towards achievement?

In the long term, a number of solutions may be available to increase our self-confidence: establishing a relationship with a mentor; training in assertiveness, interpersonal skills or stress management; possibly counselling. The demons of power-lessness and unworthiness can be critically disabling. Facing our demons can help us to conquer them.

Developing your intuition

Research and anecdote suggest that managers use intuition a great deal, but that they may not feel comfortable admitting it.

> *The final act of business judgement is intuitive.*
> Alfred Sloan

Intuition is a function of perception. It is the faculty of seeing that something may be true without objective evidence. Intuition suggests the potential contained within a situation: where something may have come from, where it may be going. It is the still small voice that tells you whether a situation 'feels good', or whether you 'smell a rat'.

Unfortunately, intuition often gives its response after the point of no return. 'That was a foolish thing to do', whispers the still small voice of calm as you plunge into a quagmire of complications that you should have seen coming. When a decision involves moral values, we call this intuitive response conscience.

As decision makers, of course, this tendency is highly inconvenient. We want intuition to work for us before the point of no return. How is this possible?

We cannot command intuition to work for us. We can, though, make ourselves more sensitive to it.

❏ When do intuitions tend to come to you? When you are closely involved with the problem? Shortly after taking a break?

❏ What state of mind best suits intuition? Relaxed? Distracted? Meditative?

❏ When do you seem to be most intuitive? On waking? Late at night? While taking exercise?

Intuition certainly needs time to do its work. Identifying precisely the 'point of no return' for a particular decision will help to take some of the stress out of your thinking and give your intuition a chance to work.

Very few decisions need to be made on the spot. It is often possible to demand time before making the decision. If possible, give yourself enough time to sleep on the problem.

Intuition often works best when we 'incubate' a problem: when we allow it to sink into our unconscious and allow intuition to go to work on it, unhindered by our conscious concerns. Incubation is a useful intuitive thinking tool. It works best when we have prepared our mind by 'worrying' at a problem, investigating it from all angles until we can go no further. Intuitive insights rarely come entirely out of the blue; they are founded on hard thinking. Sitting around waiting for inspiration will probably not work.

> *Fortune favours the prepared mind*
> Louis Pasteur

Intuition is a powerful tool in helping to manage the emotional risk of a decision. It tells us whether the decision 'feels' right or wrong – not as a value judgement, but as a statement of truth. Once our intuition is convinced of the rightness of a decision, it is as good as made – and you are already living in a new reality, transformed by the decision itself. Committing to it is now a mere formality.

The principle of engagement

When a couple commit to marry, they often announce their engagement. This is a useful test of our intuition for two reasons:

❏ It delays the point of no return. This allows intuition to work both before and after the event: to tell you whether the idea of marriage 'feels right'.
❏ It makes the commitment public. This allows others to respond to the idea – and their responses may be surprising.

A commitment does not truly exist until it is announced. The announcement is the true 'point of no return'. Some equivalent to an 'engagement' may be possible to allow you to test the water, to see what the decision 'feels like' and give others the opportunity to give their views before the decision is made. Many consultative activities will have had this effect. A pilot scheme, trial run or experiment can be useful as a form of 'engagement'.

CASE STUDY

Petra is a research officer in a national management development organization. She shows great promise and flair, and has been commissioned, not by her manager but by a director of her organization, to organize an important policy conference. She accepts the challenge although she has never organized a conference before.

It soon becomes clear to her that she is out of her depth. Policy in the issue chosen is still unclear in her own organization; it is a field beyond her immediate knowledge; the timescale is unrealistic; the work would involve liaison with senior figures from blue-chip companies.

Continued on next page

Continued from previous page

She has been in situations like this before, and met the challenge. Her reputation for pulling rabbits out of hats is what led to this commission. Now, however, her intuition tells her that this will not work.

She has become 'engaged', but no announcement has yet been made. She must act fast to prevent further complications. Uncomfortable though it is, and risking whatever may happen to her reputation, she goes straight to the director and announces that she cannot fulfil the commission.

The director accepts her apology lightly and admits that, privately, she had been unsure of her own judgement in the matter. She praises Petra for her decisiveness and puts the project on hold.

Some decisions, of course, cannot be tested before the point of no return; but it is as well to remember that confidentiality (that polite word for secrecy) may create as many problems of public response as it seeks to solve. Far too many decisions are kept secret unnecessarily, out of fear or fright.

Conversely, announcing your commitment can have surprising positive effects. You discover resources you never knew you had, and support from unexpected quarters. Until you announce the commitment, these may not have been available.

Until one is committed there is hesitancy, the chance to draw back, always ineffectiveness.

Concerning all acts of initiative (and creation), there is one elementary truth, the ignorance of which kills countless ideas and splendid plans: that the moment one definitely commits oneself, then Providence moves too. All sorts of things occur to help one that would never have otherwise occurred.

A whole stream of events issues for the decision, raising in one's favour all manner of unforeseen incidents and meetings and material assistance, which no man could have dreamt would have come his way.
W H Murray, from the Scottish Himalayan Expedition

Making use of your mistakes

Making a decision is not like solving a mathematical equation. There is no 'correct' course of action: you are designing the solution that seems most appropriate at the time.

Decisions are judged by their results. It may be better to make a wrong decision if it gets action, rather than make no decision and allow a situation to drift. If the ship is moving, you can at least correct its course.

> *Solve it. Solve it quickly, solve it right or wrong. If you solved it wrong, it would come back and slap you in the face and then you could solve it right. Lying dead in the water and doing nothing is a comfortable alternative because it is without risk, but it is an absolutely fatal way to manage a business.*
>
> Thomas J Watson Snr

The trick is to manage the risk in such a way that you can clear up any mess that you do make. And, if you do make a mistake, 'turn your regrets into gold' (to quote John Adair). Go back and try to see precisely where you went wrong. Ask what you can learn from the experience. That will put you on the alert all the sooner next time.

We learn by our mistakes. We tend not to learn so much from getting it right. Indeed, we should be making mistakes. Our errors show us where we can improve our own performance, where we need to pay attention to change in and around our organization, and where we can find opportunities to add value and enhance the quality of our services or products.

5

COMMUNICATING

Management is getting results through people. Your decision will only be successful if it is fully implemented. Communicating our decision is the primary means of implementing it.

More decisions fail because of poor communication than for any other reason. Managers often assume that the virtues of their decision are self-evident and that little needs to be done other than tell people what to do.

People will be unwilling to do anything they can see no reason for doing. Having committed to our decision, we must now generate commitment in others. How can we best do this?

❏ *Secure commitment by communicating face-to-face*
   You are selling your decision: explaining it so that people can ask questions, understand it in their terms and find a reason to accept it – even if they don't agree with it.
❏ *The responsibility for communicating the decision is yours*
   Part of your inability to commit to the decision may have been your concern about communicating it to a hostile audience. You cannot shirk that responsibility. If you do not take it, somebody else will – and probably cause even more problems.

WHOM TO COMMUNICATE WITH?

The obvious people to communicate your decision to are those who will be directly affected by it:

❏ people who will carry out the actions you have planned;
❏ those whose work will be changed by your decision;
❏ 'customers' (internal or external) who will see a difference in your products or output;
❏ sponsors who will give you support during implementation.

Finding a sponsor

Many decisions will need sponsorship if they are to survive. To implement any idea in an organization requires authority, resources (in particular, a budget) and ability. Wherever all three exist, a sphere of influence develops. Unless a decision is implemented through a sphere of influence, it is unlikely to survive.

Spheres of influence may be hard to locate. In more traditionally structured organizations, centres of power may be easy to identify – and other spheres of influence may be disguised or hidden. In 'flatter' organizations, all three elements of executive power can be spread between teams, temporary partnerships and autonomous units. Implementing decisions then becomes more complicated, involving liaison and networking.

❏ Who is making all the important decisions in your organization these days?
❏ What issues are driving the organization at the moment?
❏ What parts of the organization address those issues most directly?
❏ How relevant is your decision to those issues?
❏ What kind of authority would give our decision credibility (financial/technical/marketing/personal)?

Ideas also travel fast through what sociologists call the 'sub-cultures' of an organization: the sporting cliques, drinking clubs and social groupings where people gossip. Power operates as much through these informal structures as through the formal structures and relationships. Gaining sponsorship for a new idea may mean infiltrating and exploiting these less obvious spheres of influence.

The most powerful sponsor for your decision will be the person who can do most to help you implement it. You will recognize them by:

- ❑ their position in the organization;
- ❑ the size of their budget;
- ❑ their authority, explicit and innate;
- ❑ their status: their ability to influence others, the value placed on their expertise or opinions, their past record as people who 'make things happen'.

GAINING SPONSORSHIP

When speaking to a potential sponsor for your decision, concentrate on:

C osts

Give an estimate of how much the idea will cost, how much it will save, what the long-term financial benefits are.

H elp

How can the sponsor help? Appeal to their role as leader, coach, mentor, trainer.

I nnovation

Stress the newness of the idea. Any influential decision maker will want to be associated with new initiatives.

P restige

What is in it for them?

S ecurity

Why is the decision likely to succeed? How well are you managing the risk?

Targeting your audience

Identify, too, the 'prime movers' of your plan. In any organization, more people are likely to be involved in implementing a plan than in making it. How will they need to change their behaviour? How soon can you involve them? Have you already involved them by consulting them? What will motivate them to do what you want them to do?

FORCE FIELD ANALYSIS

Any human system – a team, a family, an organization – can be thought of as a system in a state of dynamic equilibrium. A number of forces are operating on and through the people in the system: they are constantly shifting in direction and strength, and the balance between them keeps the system relatively stable. Without the equilibrium between them, the forces in the system would tear it apart.

Implementing a new idea will change the balance of forces and threaten the system's stability. This is one reason why human beings resist being changed: they instinctively understand that change upsets the equilibrium of their social group and hence their sense of security. Pushing in the direction of change will create a pattern of resisting forces as the system tries to regain equilibrium. The system will only change the balance of forces within it if it wants to change.

We will only achieve change within the system if we can remove or lessen the forces resisting change. Force Field Analysis creates a simple, clear model of the forces supporting and opposing change.

Present situation ⟶ Desired situation

Driving forces ⟵⟶ Restraining forces

(needs, dissatisfactions, shared visions or goals)

(economic costs, fears, anxieties, politics)

personal
interpersonal
group/team/department
intergroup/team/department
organizational
administrative
technological
environmental

Continued on next page

Continued from previous page

❑ Take care to confine your analysis to a specific human system: a single team, department, managerial group or organization.
❑ Analyse the forces at work in and on the group – not in or on individuals in the group or the group conducting the analysis.
❑ Consider only the forces you can positively identify; not possible, likely or hypothetical forces.

Pursue the analysis systematically.

1. Define the change you want as specifically as possible, as it affects the group ('How to . . .').
2. As driving forces, look for:
   – needs within the group;
   – shared dissatisfactions that the change addresses;
   – shared visions of success, goals or targets.
3. As restraining forces, consider:
   – economic costs (which may not be easily quantifiable);
   – psychological costs: fears, anxieties or political opposition to the change, as well as resistance that may result from the change.
4. Address each of the restraining forces by using 'how to' thinking. Draw up plans of actions to lessen or remove each restraining force.

There are a number of general questions to ask in mapping out your action plans.

❑ What is the relative importance of the forces in the analysis? Can we quantify their relative strengths and prioritize them?
❑ Which forces do we have immediate influence on?
❑ To whom do we have immediate access?
❑ How ready is the group for change?
❑ How can we deal with the psychological costs of change sensitively?
❑ Where will we have to forge vital links between people to create change?
❑ What are the consequences on the group of failing to change?

SELLING THE DECISION

Selling a decision – to sponsors, users or 'customers' – is always a matter of persuading your audience to 'buy' it – or to 'buy into' it! Whether you are asking for support or for action, you are asking people to commit themselves to change, just as you have done.

Arguing the case for change is not a good way of selling it. Give somebody logical reasons for doing something and they will at once start to find equal and opposite reasons for not doing it! Logic creates suspicion: it can be used to justify anything, and your audience will know it.

> *You'll never convince anybody by logic alone.*
> Rudolph Flesch

What, then, will motivate people to 'buy' your decision – to commit themselves to it?

❏ Benefits to them.
❏ The evidence of their senses.
❏ A clear sense of how to proceed; the plan, rules, timescale, budget and responsibilities.

Try a bit of empathy. Put yourself into the mind of your audience.

❏ How do they see the organization and their place in it? What are their goals – short and long term? How will your decision help them to achieve those goals? What do they need – and how will the decision meet that need?

Present the decision in their terms; locate it in their network of priorities and plans. Use their language. Imagine how the decision looks from their point of view and start from there. Concentrate on how your decision will benefit them, rather than explaining every consequence. Anticipate possible objections, and acknowledge them; be sure to have an answer.

In advertising jargon: 'the eye buys'. If you can, demonstrate the effects of the decision. Use a model or a worked example; apply your decision to a real example and display the benefits. Better still, ask people to work it out for themselves.

If a practical demonstration is not possible, do the next best thing; create an evocative image in your audience's mind, which will make an immediate and lasting impression. Bring the plan of action alive by personalizing it, or by making it concrete. Use examples from real life, anecdotes, comparisons with similar situations (what happened last time; what the competition is up to; how a similar decision benefited another part of the organization).

Explain your plan of action in as much detail as necessary. Do not go into enormous detail: your task is to convince the audience that you know what you are doing and what you expect others to do – and that you have clear procedures for monitoring progress and checking against targets. If people know that you have a plan, they will feel less fearful and more secure; if you tell them too much too soon, they will only feel confused and helpless.

SELLING A DECISION: A CHECKLIST

❑ Identify your audience. You will need to sell differently to different people.
❑ Relate your decision to the audience's wider objectives and values.
❑ Sell benefits, not reasons.
❑ Demonstrate how the decision will produce the desired results.
❑ Specify the benefits in 'hard' terms.
❑ Compare costs with benefits in order to justify them.
❑ Use your audience's language.
❑ Explain your plan of action sufficiently to convince them that you know what you are doing. Explain procedures for checking and monitoring.

Different audiences will appreciate being told about decisions in different ways. Choosing the most appropriate method of communication may make the difference between success and failure.

❑ How does your audience think?
❑ What are their values?

❏ What is most important to them?
❏ What style of management do they operate?
❏ What forms of communication are they most comfortable with?

A committee may require a full written report and a presentation – even if they do not actually *need* either. A sales force will probably appreciate a conference with slides, lasers and a free lunch.

Reports and proposals

Many decisions initially appear on paper: in reports, proposals, memos or letters. Putting the decision and the proposed plan of action on paper can be useful when:

❏ you need to tell a lot of people at once;
❏ the decision or plan is complicated;
❏ you need a record for legal, contractual or administrative reasons.

The main difficulty with communicating on paper is that you may fail to communicate at all. Research suggests that most managers never read the reports that land on their desks. As organizations communicate more and more in writing – through E-mail, for example – managers are facing increasing quantities of documentation. Making your proposal stand out from all the rest may prove very difficult.

'Putting it in writing' can never be a better option than communicating a decision face-to-face. It can act, however, as a useful preparation for that conversation by briefing the audience thoroughly.

Try to time your proposal or report to appear when it will make maximum impact. If you can, avoid times when:

❏ yours is one report among many landing on your reader's desk;
❏ a bigger or more important proposal overshadows yours;
❏ holidays are looming;
❏ the financial situation is not helpful.

Your report must act in your absence. You must do everything to make your reader pick it up and read it. Package it as professionally as possible.

Remember that your reader will always have something better to do than read your report! You must make reading as easy as possible for them; and you must make them want to continue reading.

Establish the purpose of the report and your target audience. Identify your primary audience: the most important reader, without whom the decision will fail.

Work out a message for your report and place it, prominently, in your summary. Make sure that your message clearly expresses your purpose to your primary audience. Support your message with clear evidence, expressed in terms that your reader will understand.

The best reports make complexity simple. Do not give a lot of information at once: resist going into detail as much as possible. Above all, avoid telling stories: about how you came to your conclusions, the methods you used, the problems you faced. Talk about the future more than the past: concentrate on benefits, costs, implications and action plans.

Make your style assertive and forward-looking. Try not to write as you think: your reader will lose interest if they have to follow a stream of consciousness. Make a point at the head of a paragraph and use the rest of the paragraph to support it.

Presentations

Presentations – whether formal or at meetings – score over written reports and proposals because a genuine conversation becomes possible. You can communicate your enthusiasm for your decision directly to your audience; they in turn can ask questions. Presentations can generate excitement and commitment.

As a result, speaking to groups probably creates more anxiety than anything else. What if you feel less than enthusiastic? What if they ask awkward questions? Suppose they fall asleep, or turn hostile?

A presentation is a conversation in which you, the presenter, have more control than is usual. You talk; they listen (in theory, at least!). A successful presenter takes control of:

❏ the audience;
❏ the material;
❏ themselves.

Your audience will only listen if they can see a good reason to. Build your presentation, then, around the audience rather than around the material you are presenting. Speak to people rather than at them; engage them with constant and friendly eye-contact. Acknowledge their concerns as soon as possible and demonstrate that you are addressing them. Tell them what your rules are for the presentation: when they should ask questions, whether they should take notes, how long you will speak for. Use their language. Answer their questions honestly, carefully and respectfully. Make sure that, in taking questions, you do not lose control.

Keep the material as simple as possible. Your audience will forget most of it anyway. Concentrate on a small number of key points: reinforce them by repetition and concrete examples. Paint pictures in your audience's mind; build their recall.

Finally, take control of yourself by rehearsing, by having a beginning and an end that is well drilled, and by concentrating on your posture and breathing.

If you are presenting a decision at a meeting, you must prepare as rigorously as if you were making a full-blown presentation. You may have less chance of taking full control and the opportunities for losing control are far greater. Be clear what your main idea is and be ready to come to the point immediately. Know what supporting points you will make and make them. In the ensuing conversation, be ready to bring the meeting back to your main ideas – again and again if necessary.

As with a written report, avoid telling stories. Remember your overall objective: to generate commitment to a course of action.

CASE STUDY

Judith has recently been appointed as a director of a rapidly growing chain of hardware stores and makes a presentation at the company's first ever conference of store managers.

Judith is concerned at the lack of quality control in the company and wants to use the opportunity of introducing herself to the managers to announce that the chain is committed to achieving a national service quality award. She is excited by the idea – it is central to her strategy of improving the stores' performance in a difficult market, and of reducing staff turnover.

Her audience, however, is unused to conferences, management jargon and any notion that HQ might be interested in improving their lot. The announcement – made verbally by a new director of whom they know nothing – makes a minimal impact. Most store managers, after the presentation cannot even remember the name of the award. To those who can, Judith's idea sounds unrealistic and slightly patronizing.

Team briefing

Many communication problems can be overcome by installing team briefing. This ensures that decisions are transmitted down the line, from the level at which they are taken, to all the people they affect. It also ensures that the message is put over only by those who are accountable for doing so. This helps to generate commitment at every level.

Putting the message across at team briefing depends on the messenger not falling back on apologies such as 'it's not my fault, it was management's decision'. Team briefing is a good way of ensuring that managers actually manage, rather than giving excuses for not doing so.

DELEGATION

The success of your decision depends on the actions that result from it. Many of those actions will be taken by other people.

Delegation, therefore, is a vitally important part of decision making.

Delegation is deliberately choosing to give somebody authority to do something you could do yourself. It is not just 'handing out work'. You give somebody a responsibility: the task to be performed; and you devolve authority: the power to make other decisions and to take action to carry out the responsibility. Successful delegation involves matching responsibility with authority. Anybody who manages will know how difficult this can be – as will any parent or carer.

Delegation is made more difficult because the manager retains accountability. You 'carry the can'; it's your responsibility to answer for any spillages – and to mop them up!

Delegation is thus a risk. Choosing whether to delegate or not is itself a decision you will need to consider carefully. Delegating leaves you free to do your real job; it allows you to look up and ahead, to think more strategically and monitor the progress of your decision. It also generates commitment by involving and motivating people. It can give people greater job satisfaction and develop them by increasing their authority and skills.

What to delegate

Look at your plan of action and review your objectives. Identify those for which you are personally accountable.

Now distinguish between the activities you can delegate and those for which you must take personal responsibility. Obvious candidates for delegation include:

❑ routine tasks;
❑ time-consuming tasks: research, testing, administrative or co-ordinating activities;
❑ complete tasks that can be delegated as a block of work;
❑ communication tasks: letters, promotional material, telephone calls.

Delegate tasks that might be tedious for you but prove a real challenge to somebody else. A task may be time-consuming because you are not so good at it, or have no new ideas for tackling it. To somebody else, such tasks may be satisfying and rewarding, with opportunities to demonstrate creativity and high performance.

Do not delegate:

❏ tasks completely beyond the skills and experience of the person concerned;
❏ strategic, policy, confidential or security matters;
❏ tasks involving discipline over the person's peers.

Beware, too, of using any of these as excuses for not delegating. There may be other reasons for your unwillingness to delegate.

❏ *Lack of experience*
A person may appear unsuitable for a task but be highly eligible to undertake it, given appropriate support and training. It would be unwise to delegate without offering support; but the learning challenge might be precisely what makes somebody successful.

❏ *Refusing to let go*
You may enjoy certain tasks, even though they do not contribute to your core objectives. You may be frightened of letting others take authority for tasks you have always carried out in the past.

❏ *Impatience*
Others are bound to do things differently from you. They are also likely to get things wrong or seem slow to pick up skills. Performance may suffer: when did you last do something right first time? On the other hand, a fresh approach may actually improve performance. Some managers may be frightened of delegating for precisely this reason.

❏ *'Keeping in touch'*
Some managers are reluctant to delegate because they want to keep 'their finger on the pulse'. At its worst, this syndrome means that every decision must be referred to them, every letter must be countersigned by them and every mistake must be followed by a 'stewards' enquiry', at which people are criticized and humiliated in front of their colleagues.

❏ *Losing out*
Delegating responsibility and authority may lead us to feel that we are grooming our best people to leave us, that they may be promoted over our heads or that we are delegating ourselves out of a job.

All of these inhibitors can prevent you from making your decision happen, by preventing you from attending to your real responsibilities. Making yourself indispensable to the decision's success is the most likely way to cause it to fail.

Nothing is impossible for the man who doesn't have to do it himself.
A H Weiler

How to delegate

Having decided what to delegate, ask:

❏ What skills, experience, expertise and qualifications are necessary for the task?
❏ Whose skills profile best matches the need?
❏ What further training or support would be necessary?

Look for people's interest in work that they haven't done, or have maybe shown some aptitude for in unusual circumstances (covering for somebody else, coping in a crisis). Look for abilities that are exercised elsewhere: in another part of their work, perhaps outside work.

Discuss the prospect of delegating the task to the person you have chosen. If you operate a system of appraisal and target setting, this can conveniently take place at the appraisal interview.

A CONVERSATION FOR ACTION

Delegating a task is achieved through what Michael Wallaczek calls a 'conversation for action'. Such a conversation translates possibility into reality by translating intentions and plans into measurable results.

A conversation for action consists of a dynamic between requesting and promising. The manager intending to delegate makes a request:

Continued on next page

Continued from previous page

'I request that you do *x*'

❏ Give a timescale or deadline.
❏ Give conditions of satisfaction: standards or targets to be achieved, how you will monitor progress and check for success.
❏ Make it clear to the delegate that they have four possible responses.

1. They can accept the request and make a commitment: 'I promise that I will do *x* by time *y*.'
2. They can decline. A request is not an order. They must be free to say 'no', while at the same time being clear of the consequences of a refusal.
3. They can commit to commit later. 'I'll get back to you by time *z*, when I will give you a definite response.'
4. They can make a counteroffer. 'I'm not willing to do *x*; however, I am willing to promise to do *w* (or maybe part of *x*) by time *y*.'

The result of this conversation is a clear commitment by the delegate to action: to the task originally intended for delegation, to part of the task, to another task, or to refusal.

In accepting a newly delegated responsibility, the delegate must be clear about three limits on their action.

❏ *Objectives*
The broad objectives of the task, the specific targets, conditions of satisfaction and timescale should all be made explicit.
❏ *Policy*
'Rules and regulations'. The manner in which the task is carried out must conform to any legal, contractual or policy guidelines under which the organization operates.
❏ *Limits of authority*
The delegate must know clearly where their authority extends and where it ends: what powers they have for hiring or using staff, their budgetary authority, the resources available to them, their access to information, their power to take decisions without referral.

Continued on next page

Continued from previous page

Finally, the manager must give the delegate confidence to do the task. Make it plain that you will:

❑ give any support that you or they consider necessary;
❑ fund any training that may be required;
❑ be available for consultation and advice;
❑ make the delegation of the task public.

This last commitment is vital if the delegate is to do the job effectively. People are more likely to give their co-operation willingly if they know in advance that authority for a task has been delegated. If a task is being permanently handed over, remember to eliminate it from your job description and add it to the delegate's.

SHARING GOALS

Many of the action plans resulting from our decision will only be accomplished with others' help. We will need to gain the co-operation, not only of our own manager, sponsor, team or subordinates, but also of other teams or departments.

We can communicate across departmental boundaries in many ways:

❑ holding conversations: on the telephone or by visiting;
❑ setting up interdepartmental working parties or cross-functional teams (making sure that, like consultative teams, these are properly led and managed);
❑ attaching or seconding staff to other departments;
❑ holding management meetings, cross-functional meetings, training and coaching sessions.

More and more organizations are turning to project management as a way to meet the challenge of breaking through departmental barriers. Cross-functional teamwork is also essential if an organization wants to become more attuned to the needs of its customers. One of the most frequent customer complaints is that an organization's left hand does not seem to know what the right hand is doing – particularly when it is undergoing change.

Implementing a decision may well mean bringing departmental objectives into line and creating a network of support throughout the organization.

GOAL SUPPORT GRID

The Goal Support Grid is a clear means of improving communication with other managers, cross-referencing the goals of different departments and recording the agreement of support.

The grid itself charts goals against support for all departments. Attached to the grid would be a number of pages containing:

❑ details of the objectives of each department (one department per page);
❑ lists of the support to be provided from one department to another for each goal, numbered in line with the numbers on the grid.

Goal support grid

	Dept. A	Dept. B	Dept. C	Dept. D
Dept. A	(A's goals see p. 2)	3, 4, 16	1, 19, 12	8, 10
Dept. B	2, 7, 11	(B's goals see p. 3)	9	20
Dept. C	5, 6, 13	3, 18	(C's goals see p. 4)	nil
Dept. D	nil	3, 5, 17	9	(D's goals see p. 5)

To complete the grid, follow the 'goal support drill'.

1. Work out the goals and actions involved in implementing your decision.
2. Identify which goals need the help of other managers or departments. How much help do you need?

Continued on next page

Continued from previous page

3. Explain these to your colleagues, either at a joint meeting or one-to-one.
4. Agree the support needed from each colleague in turn: specific actions, targets and deadlines.
5. Your colleagues will themselves have goals requiring support. Encourage them to explain them and agree the support you can give each other. Seek a *quid pro quo* if possible: do not be afraid to negotiate.
6. Resolve incompatible goals or duplicated support. Refer up to the next level of management if necessary.
7. Set a date for review.

The goal support drill can quickly become integrated as an operational standard for the management team. Each new decision will form part of regular review and update of the grid.

Using the grid has a number of benefits.

❏ Each manager has a clearer idea of their colleagues' objectives.
❏ Each manager is committed to providing specific support and to expect support in return.
❏ Everybody saves time. Meetings can be called for those who are involved in a particular objective, rather than large numbers of people who are not needed.
❏ The managers' manager can use the grid to check for spare capacity or work overload. They can urge the 'I've-only-got-time-for-my-own-problems' manager to greater co-operation, and the more relaxed managers to 'keep their eye on the ball'.
❏ The grid can help to sharpen objectives and set clear targets at appraisal or performance review.
❏ Managers can budget more effectively, by agreeing to contribute something measurable as support. An objective requiring an income of £x could be achieved by department A contributing 80 per cent, leaving department B to support by contributing 15 per cent and department C 5 per cent.
❏ The drill does not have to be implemented in a whole department or area. Managers do not even need the support of their leaders to carry it out (though such sponsorship certainly helps). The goal support grid is evidence of true cross-functional co-operation.

6

CHECKING

We can measure the success of any decision only by its results.

Those results will be achieved by people: primarily those you manage, your team, and other teams; but also your suppliers and customers, internal or external. You can obtain a great deal of information through the normal channels: from team briefings, from sales figures and statistics. You can also find out a great deal from walking the job: going to see for yourself how people are getting on. And you can judge results most effectively by setting targets and observing how the results measure up against them.

Checking, however, is never merely 'checking up' on people! Monitoring progress against objectives involves more than calling for the numbers every month, just as 'management by walking about' is more than dropping in unannounced or 'spying' on people. Bald statistics can be misleading; and if your team feels that you are prying 'for no reason', they are less likely to give you the information you need to assess how well they are doing.

People will produce excellent results if they are motivated to achieve them. All the processes of checking our decisions – deciding performance indicators, setting targets, measuring progress, identifying development needs – work best if we *involve* our team in them.

Checking our decision, then, integrates our decision making skills into our wider responsibilities as managers. It places our decisions in the context of the work of the teams we manage. And it is an essential part of our own learning cycle. Reviewing a decision helps us plan the *next* decision – and improve our skills as decision makers.

MONITORING PERFORMANCE

Your decision will change the way people work. It may have implications for job descriptions, appraisal, the criteria for performance-related pay or reward. The decision's success will be determined by many factors. Checking how it is working out will only be effective if you have some way of knowing objectively what is happening. Monitoring performance is the process of comparing what is happening against clear targets.

It is vital that we can make the comparison in a *measurable* way. Only by having objective measures can we agree how well we are doing. Those measures must be directly related to our objectives in making the decision. We can only measure what happens, so we must measure results and behaviour – what people do and achieve, rather than their personality or attitude.

> *If you don't know where you are going, you will probably end up somewhere else.*
>
> Laurence J Peter

Begin by asking two key questions:

❏ 'What am I trying to achieve?'
❏ 'How will I know that I've achieved it?'

Answering the first question will identify your *objective*; answering the second will help you to establish the *key result areas* within which you can measure progress.

Objectives are broad directions in which you want to travel. They are similar to trends, describing movement (in contrast to a target, which is a desired point of arrival). 'To maximize profit', 'to minimize waste', 'to optimize use of equipment' – all are examples of objectives in this sense.

Key result areas are those within which we want to improve performance. They should reflect your business activities and the organization's broader mission: why it exists. They are useful in many ways: they will help you set targets, measure individuals' progress against them and identify opportunities to develop people's skills. They can be the agenda headings for team briefings or performance reviews. You will probably not need more than half a dozen.

KEY RESULT AREAS:
some examples from different organizations

Product quality: Costs; production time; staff involvement; customer satisfaction
(food manufacturer).

Shareholder value: Product quality; production efficiency; wastage; delivery time; customer satisfaction
(car manufacturer).

Service quality: Costs; performance against schedules; safety; customer care
(public transport company).

Leadership: Service quality; application processing time; team working; return on investments
(housing association).

It will be important to define these headings in terms that are specific to your organization or team. Everybody must understand what you mean by them – including you!

We can measure progress in key result areas by using *performance indicators*: yardsticks that tell us *what to measure* in order to plot our progress against targets.

PERFORMANCE INDICATORS
(and some examples)

❑ **Percentages/ratios**

   Attendance rate to achieve 97.3 per cent

❑ **Frequency of occurrence**

   Hold a minimum of ten meetings a year to review targets.

Continued on next page

Continued from previous page

❏ **Averages**

Achieve an average of 70 per cent unit productivity over the year.

❏ **Time**

Respond to all call-outs within three hours.

❏ **Prohibition**

No service to be cancelled because of parts shortages.

❏ **External standards**

Achieve favourable Health and Safety Executive report.

Having established how you will measure success in achieving your objectives, you can set *targets*. These are measurable or fixed points that you can aim for in our pursuit of objectives. People sometimes resist the idea of setting targets, perhaps because too much importance is given to them as signs of success or failure – and because reward is often based on them.

We must keep target setting in perspective. If we want to measure progress, we must have a means of measuring it. If we want to go further, and *motivate* ourselves to achieve progress, a target can be very useful. Setting targets will help you to:

❏ focus your activities;
❏ measure improvement or progress;
❏ establish a firm basis for any reward or bonuses;
❏ motivate your team to achieve excellence and greater attention to detail.

Targets are not sacred. Whether we achieve our targets will depend, not only on our own performance, but on other factors outside our control. What we really need to know is whether people are moving in the right direction: whether they continue to be focused on objectives. Targets can help us make that judgement. But it can be all too easy to sacrifice improvements in performance on the altar of targets: to destroy people's motivation to do better, in the relentless pursuit of numbers.

We should set targets, then, that will encourage people to achieve. They should never become a burden by being too difficult or too detailed. On the basis of these targets, we can review performance, which, in turn, will allow us to assess people's *competencies*: the skills, behaviours and aptitudes that are required to perform the task. That assessment then forms the starting point for people's development.

How to establish performance review

Performance review is a formalized system of checking progress against targets. These ten steps will help you to set up a review procedure that gives a wide range of benefits, helping you to manage performance, motivate your team and develop people's competence.

Your organization may have already taken a number of these steps. A mission statement, for example, will indicate how your objectives align to wider goals; team briefing is a valuable system for sharing goals and reviewing performance. It is important that, at every step, you *involve* your team as much as possible.

1. Establish the purpose of the action you have decided to take.
2. Decide what team objectives will contribute to this purpose: the direction you will move in as a team.
3. Identify the key result areas within which those objectives are located.
4. Establish the performance indicators by which you will measure progress towards objectives. Set targets. Align these with measures for team reward or bonuses as appropriate.
5. Repeat steps 2–4 for individuals. Ensure no overlaps in action responsibilities, and that lines of liaison, support and co-operation are clear.
6. Set up the review procedures:
   - one-to-ones to review performance, set new targets and develop people;
   - regular team meetings to share goals and targets, feed back on progress and reinforce your original decision;

       – walking the job to see what is happening as it happens and monitor progress informally.

7. Identify the competencies necessary to carry out the work: the behaviours, skills, and capabilities people need to pursue objectives and hit targets. Cross reference these against key result areas and performance indicators, so that you can:
       – check the effectiveness of the indicators;
       – improve job descriptions;
       – align personal development to the needs of the work.

8. Establish the competencies already possessed by team and team members. New team members may be required if your decision demands radically new competencies.

9. Draw up a development programme for individual team members to develop their skills.

10. Organize the training, coaching, mentoring, opportunities and other methods for development. You may need training yourself, in:
       – objective setting;
       – target setting;
       – coaching, appraisal or mentoring;
       – team building;
       – team briefing or team performance review.

MONITORING PERFORMANCE

What is your objective?

Identify key result areas

Establish performance indicators within
each key result area

Set targets

Review performance against targets

Assess and review competencies

Draw up development plan

It is important that, at every step, you *involve* your team as much as possible, not simply tell them what you have decided to monitor. Ask what objectives people have for their own work; examine how those fit in with your goals and the wider goals of the organization. Ask, too, what contribution people can make to meet those objectives. Use their knowledge of customers, systems, procedures, and how the job is done best. Focus on the improvements that your decision is designed to create. If you have consulted earlier in the decision making process, consultation on review will be much easier.

Gaining such involvement requires more than managerial skill. It requires leadership. People must be empowered to contribute to the whole process of performance review. We take ownership of challenges that we have participated in setting ourselves. At the same time, your task is to manage the process – not merely reactively by becoming obsessed with statistics, but proactively by setting the task, explaining the context, and encouraging people to do their best.

> *Managers accomplish tasks and take responsibility; leaders influence others and translate vision into action.*
>
> Warren Bennis

Beware of management by numbers. Performance indicators are precisely that: indicators of performance, and no more. Do not be tempted to use them as a means of *enforcing* performance improvements. Similarly, beware of 'cascading'. By making a decision, you have chosen and committed to a course of action. Do not jeopardize the situation by slotting implementation mechanically into the objectives and targets dictated by senior management. You should be involving people in setting their own objectives, not allocating a basket of higher level objectives and targets piecemeal. If necessary, translate the higher-level goals into your own language, and that of the team, so that people understand their relevance to them.

Getting the words right

The language of performance review can cause a lot of confusion.

What is the difference between an objective, a goal and a target? Are key results the same as key measures? Or are key measures actually performance indicators?

Such confusion can be made worse when people from different organizations – or different parts of the same organization – use the same vocabulary in different ways. A 'strategic objective' at divisional level can become a series of 'departmental goals' at another.

Use your own language. Do not introduce a new set of terms unnecessarily. Confusion over words can create doubt about the people using them; and cynicism preys on doubt. If your organization has a total quality programme, it will probably already be using many of the words of performance management. If not, clarify the terms you are using with your team to ensure that everybody knows what they are talking about.

The terms we use in this book – objective, key result area, performance indicator, target, competency – have other names in other circumstances. Use whatever is appropriate in your situation, remembering that performance review is a matter of knowing where you are going, where you want to see improvement, how you intend to measure that improvement, and what you will challenge yourself to achieve on the road to success.

Objective

Where you want to go. The direction you want to travel. Expressed in terms of movement rather than results: *maximize, minimize, optimize.* Also known as corporate goals (or objectives), divisional goals or strategic objectives.

Key result area

Where we want to see success or improvement. Sometimes known as key measures, key headings or key values.

Performance indicator

The means by which we measure our success in pursuing our objectives in the key result areas.

Target

Points on the road to success. Also known as goals or milestones. Identifiable and measurable in terms of the performance indicators.

Competency

The behaviours, skills and capabilities required to do the job: to pursue the objectives and hit targets.

Setting targets

You make decisions as part of your quest for improved performance. Targets are points on your journey that tell you whether you are going in the right direction, at the right speed.

Setting targets, then, is a regular activity. Because you will be doing it often, it makes sense not to set too many. Look back at your decision; review your objectives; ask what you need to know to assess how successful the decision has been in improving performance.

Begin by asking:

❑ 'What are we trying to do?'
❑ 'Who is involved?'
❑ 'What, specifically, do we have to do to meet our objective?'
❑ 'What are the action responsibilities for:
   – me;
   – team members;
   – the team as a whole;
   – other people: teams, departments, customers or suppliers?'
❑ 'When are the deadlines?'
❑ 'Which organizational objectives is this decision supporting?'
   (It may be contributing to more than one)
❑ 'Which of our customers' objectives are we supporting?'
❑ 'How do we measure success?'

Targets should be SMART:

❑ **S**pecific.
❑ **M**easurable.

❏ **Agreed** with the jobholder.
❏ **Realistic.**
❏ **Time-related.**

They should be SMART primarily for the people who will have to try to hit them. A measurable target for you may seem very vague to somebody else; an achievable target for one person can be a nightmare for another. People should, at the very least, know how and why you are setting targets for them. Far better, try to involve them in setting the targets themselves and explain how you intend to monitor them.

Involving people in setting their own targets has numerous advantages.

❏ You are more likely to get the co-operation vital to success.
❏ The jobholder knows more about the job or task than anybody else.
❏ The jobholder is more likely to take ownership of a challenge they have helped to set.
❏ Collective involvement will help to maintain good employee relations.

Do not try to set too many targets at once. Concentrate on what will help to make your decision work: the biggest, the most central, the most urgent. Measure only what will demonstrate success in those areas.

Be precise enough to avoid disagreement over whether the target has been hit. Measure output rather than input: the number of units produced rather than the number of hours worked, for example. Keep deadlines as short as possible, given the nature of the target. Consider staggering deadlines to give the jobholder more chance of meeting them.

Real targets for real people must motivate them to do better. So:

❏ quantify them in terms of key result areas;
❏ make them achievable but challenging;
❏ set targets in areas over which the jobholder has control;
❏ explain how they support wider goals and higher-level organizational objectives;

❑ involve the jobholder in setting them;
❑ set a realistic timetable;
❑ concentrate on whatever will improve *performance*; not merely routine activities.

Beware of changing targets suddenly: in a crisis, for example, or for a reason that isn't apparent to the jobholder. But do be willing to alter a target if it turns out over time to be unrealistic, or if external circumstances conspire to make it unachievable.

Overcoming resistance

Involving people in target setting and performance review will always create the possibility of resistance. If change becomes ever more unpredictable and people feel less and less secure, any change – and any decision – affecting them can fuel uncertainty and defensiveness.

Some people may feel that their work cannot be measured numerically, or that their work is entirely reactive and dependent on others: receptionists, helpline operators or customer care staff; production line staff assembling parts to a pre-set programme. Others will thrive on confusion: the moment they see others unsure of the task, or muddled over terms, they will use the opportunity to foment hostility. Others again may have seen initiatives come and go and have grown a hard crust of cynicism to protect themselves from the latest 'management fad'.

Such feelings are more likely to emerge in a group discussion than in one-to-one conversations – and to be amplified as remark piles on top of remark. A team meeting can easily turn into an uncontrolled 'grouse session' that does more harm than good.

Be prepared. If you are leading a meeting that is in danger of becoming a forum for group resistance, arm yourself with a few guiding principles.

❑ Make the objective of the meeting clear at the outset. Write it up on a flip chart and be ready to refer back to it frequently. Challenge people to explain the relevance of their remarks to the meeting's objectives.

❏ Remember that your task is to control the discussion. Do not be drawn into the emotional maelstrom.

❏ Do not interrupt or cut people off in mid-sentence.

❏ Listen to the points people are making and display them openly, on the flip chart.

❏ Stop people from talking about others who are not at the meeting. Insist that 'they' are not here and we are, and that only we can address our objectives.

❏ Do not be tempted to argue, or to contradict opinions or generalizations: about what 'they' do, or what 'always' happens. A good response to such remarks would be: 'So what are *we* trying to do?'

❏ Turn complaints into objectives by asking people to restate them as 'how to' statements. Write these up on the flipchart and display them.

❏ Focus on solutions, not problems.

❏ Be a broken record! Repeat your questions to the group, over and over – 'What are we trying to do? What can *we* do about it? How does this relate to our objectives?'

Confusion and doubt are best dealt with by being specific. People should know what contribution they are being asked to make, and how their contribution will contribute to wider objectives. Being explicit about goals and targets is the only way to achieve this. If you genuinely consult – asking for suggestions, inviting people to participate in the process – a great deal of resistance will melt away.

> *An employee without information cannot take responsibility. With information, he or she cannot avoid taking it.*
> Jan Carlzon, SAS Airline

Focus on *action*. Resistance to an initiative often centres on what has happened in the past, and in particular on what 'they' have done: senior management, other teams, department heads, 'rogue operators' who have bucked the system, engineers or sales staff who are never in the office, customers, suppliers, competitors... Draw the group's attention away from what others have done or are doing, towards *what we will do in the future.*

You will have to be sensitive about this. Demonstrating that you understand people's grievances can be useful in winning them over to your own ideas – and in rooting out areas for improvement. But there will come a point in a 'grouse session' when you should start asking, insistently but quietly: 'So what are we going to do?' In this way, you will divert attention from damaging 'storytelling' and fruitless complaint towards commitment and agreement. By showing that something *can* be done, you can give people hope that they have power to change things; by agreeing ways of measuring what they do, people can begin to feel less reactive and more proactive.

In particular, you should be prepared for arguments such as:

❑ 'It's just making us work harder for no extra money.'
❑ 'You're giving us management responsibilities that aren't in our job descriptions.'
❑ 'It's just a new way of passing the blame onto us.'
❑ 'Management are riding roughshod over established agreements and contracts.'
❑ 'We've always done it this way – why should we change?'
❑ 'This will waste our time doing irrelevant things.'
❑ 'Management moving the goalposts again!'

Record these and other points, and then turn the discussion around by asking: 'What are the four or five points that would tell you whether you'd had a good week or a bad week?'

Typical replies might be:

❑ 'I didn't get any complaints.'
❑ 'I got more complaints than ever before.'
❑ 'We had to change the production schedule in mid-cycle and wasted time and resources.'
❑ 'The engineer was slow to repair the kit and I had to work overtime to clear the backlog.'
❑ 'We received 100 per cent customer satisfaction ratings for the first time ever.'
❑ 'Every delivery happened within 24 hours.'

People are now referring to *results*. Good times and bad times are almost always related to output, which is measurable in some way. They will usually also relate to divisional or organizational goals. As a manager, you can demonstrate these relationships and show how people's sense of achievement is directly linked to the organization's objectives.

Categorize responses in terms of key result areas and ask how such achievements can be measured. Lead on to discuss performance indicators and use them to draw up targets.

❏ Ask: 'How do you recognize success in your work?'
❏ Ask: 'How could we measure that element of success?'
❏ Explain how your decision helps to achieve or register such success.
❏ How do these measures of success relate to wider objectives? Why are we in business? What are we trying to do?
❏ Objectives are more important than targets. Targets shift; objectives will tend to remain fixed for longer. Our quest is for continuous improvement; the target only helps us to go in the right direction.

Your responsibility as a manager is to help your organization go where it wants to go, to be clear where you are going and to help others to set their sights clearly. That is why you make the decisions you make. Setting objectives and targets helps everybody involved to go in the same general direction. Some targets will not be met; others we will hit a little too easily. Hence the need for constant review and adjustment. And hence the need for more decisions!

This is your answer if people accuse you of 'moving the goalposts'. Shifting targets is part of the job. We live in a world of shifting goalposts and the pursuit of excellence never stops.

FOLLOWING PEOPLE'S PROGRESS

We monitor performance:

❏ to assess the effectiveness of our decision in action;
❏ to review performance against targets;
❏ to review the targets themselves;

❏ if necessary, to set new targets;
❏ to help develop people.

There are three main ways of assessing how people are doing: one-to-one interviews; team performance reviews; and walking the job.

One-to-ones

One-to-ones should be frequent: at least once a month. Informal conversations are always useful for keeping track of progress – if they concentrate on work rather than 'gossip' or 'the feel-good factor'. Make time for more formal reviews as well.

Appraisals are the most formal of such conversations and are usually held annually. Half-yearly appraisals are becoming more common.

Set aside time for a one-to-one. Do not spring them on people unannounced, and take care not to give the impression that you are permanently spying! The best way of demonstrating that you trust people to use their initiative, after all, is to trust them to use their initiative.

The aim of a one-to-one will be to review performance against targets and broader objectives. Do not feel you have to review every target every time: some will be more urgent than others.

❏ Ask the jobholder in advance whether they wish to talk about anything and explain any issues you want to discuss. Draw up an informal agenda. There should be no surprises.
❏ Create a relaxed and quiet situation. Take notes, and invite the jobholder to do the same.
❏ Have targets been met? If so, what can we learn from them?
❏ If they have not been met, why?
  – failure of performance: time management, lack of skill, lack of focus?
  – failure on your part to provide resources, support or explanation?
  – circumstances beyond our control: sickness, extra work, systems failures ... ?
❏ If the target has not been met, can we extend the deadline or

find another way of achieving it? Should we consider it irrelevant?
❏ How is the jobholder managing routine parts of the job?
❏ Identify successes and failures. Set new targets if necessary.
❏ Be constructive and talk at least as much about the future as about the past. Concentrate on achievement rather than attitude or personality.
❏ Review competencies: skills and behaviours needed to achieve targets and improve achievements.
❏ Seek agreement, to ensure that the jobholder takes ownership of targets. In the last resort, you have a duty to tell somebody what you require of them; but agreement is more powerful as a motivator than instruction.
❏ Keep the conversation short. Summarize frequently, and at the end. Review how the working relationship is developing.
❏ After the one-to-one, take notes and let the jobholder have a copy. Consider how your decision is working out. Resist any temptation to change course in a hurry.

The worst mistake a boss can make is not to say 'well done'.
John Ashcroft

Team performance review

Team performance review allows people to see how they are working together. It helps a team to focus on its objectives and allows people to remember how their individual action responsibilities fit into the larger plan developed to implement your decision.

Team performance review:

❏ helps to manage change;
❏ reinforces teamwork;
❏ raises team commitment to your decision;
❏ reduces the possibility of misunderstanding;
❏ combats the effect of the 'grapevine';
❏ monitors morale;
❏ builds trust.

It is a development of team briefing, where a senior management brief is 'cascaded' through a team leader to their team. In a performance review, the team shares objectives and targets, and gives feedback on its performance. As team leader, you can also use the meeting to feed back your impressions of how things are going, and relate the team's work to that of other terms. You can even use it to ask the team how they think *you* are doing!

Hold team performance reviews regularly: not just in a crisis, or when things are going badly. Monthly reviews are common. Ensure that the whole team attends (you may wish to hold two meetings if the team is of more than 20 people, if certain operations must be covered constantly or if you operate in shifts).

❑ Hold the meeting at the beginning of the working day or shift.
❑ Hold it always in paid time.
❑ The review should last between 10 and 40 minutes.
❑ Hold the review at the workplace, in a quiet area away from phones and other interruptions.
❑ Create a friendly, positive atmosphere.

Team performance review should be exactly that: a discussion about how we are doing and what we can do collectively to improve performance. Such meetings have measurable benefits. If it is not about performance, productivity, qualities and quantities, it will be a waste of time.

Cover the 'Four Ps':

❑ *Progress.* Our achievements. Include individual achievements if appropriate. Reflect back to the team what we have done so far to reach our goals, how the decision is working out. Start with progress because it helps to create a positive feeling in the team.
❑ *Policy.* How developments elsewhere in the organization are affecting what we are doing.
❑ *People.* Any relevant matters affecting team members that will strengthen the team.
❑ *Points for action.* What we need to do in the future. Any new targets, or special points for action. If you are introducing a new decision to the team, this would be the place to do it.

When you present a new decision at a team performance review, plan your presentation carefully. Make sure the team is tightly organized and anticipate any likely questions. Use your language and the team's vocabulary – not that of senior management or 'organizationspeak'. Announce your decision and explain the reasons for it; give concrete examples to supply your ideas and use visual aids to explain them; answer questions honestly or arrange to answer them later. (Further advice on selling a decision is in Chapter 5.)

Walking the job

By going out and walking the job, you can observe your plan of action *in action*. Only by seeing for yourself can you follow progress 'as it happens' and be *seen* to be keeping in touch.

Walking the job – or 'management by walking about' – gives you the opportunity to discuss individual and team achievements, ideas and problems (or 'issues'). Benefits to you include:

❑ Finding out what is going on: seeing and hearing people at work and listening to their views firsthand.
❑ Getting answers and comments from people that would not emerge in a more formal interview or meeting.
❑ Strengthening your image with the team as interested, approachable and – above all – *committed* to success.
❑ Keeping people on track, thanking, praising, encouraging and stimulating them.

Benefits for the team include:

❑ The chance to speak directly to you.
❑ The opportunity to relate what they are doing to wider objectives.

If walking the job seems an artificial or awkward style of management, you probably need to try it at once. There is no substitute for making direct, face-to-face contact with the team carrying out your plan of action. It will develop your skill at fostering effective teamwork and help you catch the first tell-tale signs of a potential crisis. Above all, walking the job demonstrates your commitment to others and helps to generate commitment in them.

WALKING THE JOB: A CHECKLIST

DO

❏ Set aside time.
❏ Explain clearly why you are there.
❏ Plan to cover everybody within a defined period.
❏ Try to find out in advance whether there are particular concerns about progress or implementation.
❏ Make sure that you speak to everybody.
❏ Talk primarily about the job.
❏ Be positive – particularly in the face of complaints or 'whinges'.
❏ Use first names.
❏ Note issues that people raise and plan your response.
❏ Be honest.
❏ Listen.

DON'T

❏ Speak to the same people every time.
❏ Answer questions you have no authority to answer.
❏ Speak on behalf of other managers.
❏ Make up answers.
❏ Appear to be 'checking up' or fault-finding.
❏ Appear to be in a hurry.
❏ Criticize in public.
❏ Tell people what to do unless they ask you to.

If your decision is working, walking the job helps you identify good practice and generate commitment by 'catching people doing things right'. Praise is the very best form of motivation.

If the decision is not working, walk the job to establish the possible causes:

❏ inadequate information or briefing;
❏ poor judgement;
❏ lack of courage;
❏ inadequate planning;
❏ lack of commitment from management (or from you).

Identifying what is going wrong is the first step towards finding improvements. Very few major managerial decisions work out perfectly. As a result of walking the job – and monitoring progress in other ways – we can evaluate what can be done to 'correct the course of the ship':

❑ whether we can improve our preparation or consultation methods;
❑ how we can communicate and brief people better;
❑ where and how people need to be trained;
❑ where we can improve standards or quality;
❑ how we can delegate further;
❑ whether and how we might reward good work;
❑ what we can do to put things right.

DEVELOPING PEOPLE

Your decisions will change the way people work, giving them new responsibilities, challenges and opportunities. To meet these, they will have to develop their *competencies*: the skills and behaviours that will lead to improved results.

We can only develop ourselves. Only by helping people take responsibility for their own development can we achieve the improved performance we require. Assessing and building competence is a matter for co-operation between manager and jobholder.

> *The door to development is locked with the key on the inside.*
>
> Peter Honey

Competencies are *not* character or personality traits. Neither are they 'attitudes'. We are seeking to develop what people do, rather than what they are.

Typical lists of managerial competencies will include:

❑ planning;
❑ problem solving;
❑ budgetary control;
❑ setting objectives;

❏ face-to-face communication;
❏ written communication;
❏ developing individuals;
❏ team building;
❏ customer relationships;
❏ self-development.

For non-managerial staff, the list may include:

❏ knowledge of the job;
❏ quality of work;
❏ ability to hit targets;
❏ interpersonal skills;
❏ response to supervision;
❏ initiative and adaptability;
❏ motivation and commitment;
❏ orderliness and administrative ability;
❏ self-presentation;
❏ punctuality;
❏ safety consciousness and first-aid skills;
❏ customer relationships.

Each competency will be described in terms of 'core activities' that are necessary to demonstrate competence, specific tasks that contribute to those activities, and identifiable activities that produce the best performance in the competency. These lists will be cross-referenced to job descriptions and can be assessed in one-to-ones or at appraisal.

Assessing somebody's competence in a particular area is not a matter of trying to produce a 'company clone'. It is a technique for identifying the support, training and coaching that will help them develop in their work. Encourage people to assess their own competencies before discussing them with you. Make your own assessment and then, openly and honestly, compare notes. On the basis of the comparison, you can begin to plan further development.

You can highlight the most important areas for development by cross-referencing the competencies required to the job against key result areas. Where a competency contributes fundamentally to a key result area, mark it for special consideration. Where it is essential for a job's effectiveness, or a task's success, mark it twice.

Relate your assessments always to the work and to the tasks in hand, and particularly to any changes that your decision has made necessary. If you allocate marks for levels of competence, always discuss these with the jobholder. Identify areas of agreement and put them to one side. Identify areas where you can agree a need for development and discuss how they might be addressed. Identify areas of disagreement and talk them through; if necessary, seek external or specialist advice (from Personnel or your Human Resource department).

Having agreed the competencies you need to address, begin to draw up a development plan. This should aim to:

❏ redress performance that resulted in failure to meet targets;
❏ strengthen competencies that are critical to the job;
❏ develop competencies that are important in key result areas;
❏ consolidate competencies that are already well developed.

Formal training is not the only way to develop people. Create opportunities for the jobholder to practise a competency: project work, specific tasks that can usefully be delegated. Make yourself available for coaching (a much cheaper option than a formal training course!). On occasions, it can be useful to set up a mentoring relationship with a manager or colleague elsewhere in the organization.

Helping the people in your team to develop takes us beyond decision making into other areas of managerial skill. As decision makers, we are coming full circle. Monitoring performance against targets gives us a clear idea of how well our decision is working out. Complete success or failure is unlikely: some parts of a decision will have been successful; others will require adjustment. In extreme circumstances, we may even have to act to overturn a decision with the next one.

Every decision is provisional. We make the best decisions we can at the time. Until they are put into practice, we cannot know whether they are good decisions or not. Reviewing their effects in measurable ways puts us in a better position to prepare for future decisions – and to develop our decision-making skills.

AFTERWORD

As I was finishing this book, my daughter was given a new story book. In it, Toad begins his day by deciding what to do and making a list: 'wake up', 'eat breakfast', 'get dressed' and so on. One of his things to do is take a walk with Frog. On their walk, the wind rips the list out of Toad's hand and it blows away.

'Hurry!' cries Frog. 'We'll run and catch it.'

'No! I can't do that,' replies Toad. 'Running after my list isn't on my list of things to do.'

We tend to think of decisions as final. The word itself derives from a Latin stem meaning 'to cut' (like *incision* or *precision*). Our mental model of a decision is of a single event in time, after which we cut off all further consideration of the matter. To be decisive, according to this model, is to take *control*: to have command of the facts, to weigh the options, to choose the best solution, and to stick to it – however the wind blows.

No wonder that so many managers feel that indecisiveness is a weakness to be overcome. To be decisive is to be strong; the ability to grapple with reality and bend it to our will is seen as a sign of power. The image of the commanding, heroic manager is enormously influential: it is the stuff of which business legends are made. Indecision, by contrast, is seen as 'hedging', 'wavering' or 'dithering': letting events control *us* – and is viewed with scorn.

The fetish of 'control' haunts all our decision making. We try to control reality in two ways: by using rational analysis to understand it, and power – or force – to change it. Most established decision-making techniques encourage us to reinforce our control by using analytical tools, focusing on specific aspects of a situation, checking, quantifying and demanding unequivocal outcomes. You have seen some of these tools and techniques in this book.

Sometimes such an approach is appropriate. Faced with the task of choosing between half a dozen different products or systems, and an increasing mountain of information about them, it makes sense to stop investigating and start analysing. Faced with a crisis, it makes sense to stop consulting and order all hands to the pumps.

Other decisions, however, cannot be tackled in this way. They are fuzzy, wicked or vicious: the parameters are unclear, they cannot be proved effective until they are implemented, or they involve other people. Many of our most important decisions are of this kind: hiring and firing; timing important announcements; whether to invest more resource in a project or abandon it; whether (and how) to restructure or promote change in an organization; and so on.

Such situations are too complicated to read clearly. They include elements that cannot be understood entirely rationally: rumour, anxiety, resistance. Faced with such complexity, we cannot easily predict the implications of any decision. Because the decision will be implemented over time and have repercussions in many different areas, no solution can ever be unarguably 'the right one'.

Rational decision making seeks to reduce three fundamental aspects of reality that Richard Pascale calls 'existential givens':

❑ *ambiguity* (about what somebody or something means);
❑ *uncertainty* (about the outcomes of events);
❑ *imperfection* (in ourselves, in others, in the initial situation and in results).

Committing to a course of action without acknowledging these factors can be dangerous. Forcing the issue will undoubtedly produce results; and if our organization demands results *now*, we will do whatever produces results – any results, at whatever cost. But seeking to exert control through an alliance of rational analysis and power may also result in outcomes that are counterproductive.

We must revise our traditional mental model of decisions. Organizational reality *is* ambiguous, uncertain and imperfect most of the time: to make decisions on the basis of eliminating these factors from our thinking may be less than useful, *particularly when the decision involves or affects other people.*

In this book I have presented a different mental model. Making decisions, according to this model, is the process, not of solving problems but of *designing solutions*: designs that help us towards our objectives while accommodating uncertainty; that exist in time and so are subject to continuous review; that can never be perfect and can always be improved. Being decisive becomes a matter of exerting *influence*, rather than power, over the flow of events. It is a question of deciding whether to decide, or whether to try to move forward. Effective action in complex situations requires us to be tentative, sensitive and keenly alert.

Human beings – and organizations – crave change, but we also crave stability. Balancing those two demands in the decisions you make will require the very best of you. Perhaps good decision making involves the recognition of a paradox: that we must always be firmly committed to temporary solutions. Making a decision is committing to a course of action – and committing to change.

BIBLIOGRAPHY

Adair, John (1985) *Management decision making*, Gower, Aldershot.

Barker, Alan (1995) *Creativity for managers*, The Industrial Society, London.

de Bono, Edward (1993) *Teach your child to think*, Penguin, London.

Brown, Rob & Brown, Margaret (1994) *Empowered!*, Nicholas Brealey, London.

Forrest, Andrew (1989) *Delegation*, The Industrial Society, London.

Heirs, Ben (1989) *The professional decision thinker*, Grafton, London.

Majaro, Simon (1992) *Managing ideas for profit*, McGraw-Hill, Maidenhead.

Moores, Roger (1994) *Managing for high performance*, The Industrial Society, London.

Rickards, Tudor (1990) *Creativity and problem solving at work*, Gower, Aldershot.

Senge, Peter (1992) *The fifth discipline*, Century Business, London.

INDEX

action 15, 16, 22, 41, 45, 49, 70, 71, 127
  assessing consequences of 52–6
  choosing 57–8
  conversation for 67, 106–8
  delegating 103–8
  planning 30, 48, 74, 76, 108–10
  reviewing 128–30
  securing 93–4, 95–6, 98–103, 117, 122
Adair, J 10, 91
adversarial thinking 68–9
advocacy and enquiry, balancing 70–2
alternatives 19, 29, 31
  appraisal criteria 50–2
  eliminating 49–59
  generating 45–9
appraisals 125
Argyris, C 39, 70
Ashcroft J 126
authority, managerial 25–6, 28, 62–3, 65–6, 79, 80

backwards planning 43–4
Bennis, W 117
brain, left- and right-12
brainstorming 77–8

Carlzon, J 122
checking 12, 13, 30, 111–33
commitment, securing 93
committing 12, 13, 15–16, 30, 79–91
  definition 79
  difficulties of 80–1, 84
  emotional 83–7
  and engagement 89–90
communicating 12, 13, 30, 93–110
  whom with 93–7
competency 115, 116, 118, 119, 126, 130
  developing 130–3
consequences, assessing 52–6
considering 12, 29–30, 31–59
consulting 12, 13, 30
  by conversation 66–73
  dangers of 64–5
  and participating 61–4
  in teams 73–8
  whom to consult 65–6
conversation
  for action 106–8
  conflict in 68–9
  to consult 66–8
  dynamics of 70
  managing 67–8, 70–2
  for opportunity 67

for possibility 67
for relationship 67
creativity 47–8
    'abrasion' 68
    metaphorical excursions 47
    oracle 48
    rule reversal 47
culture, organizational 19, 26–7,
        46, 50, 70, 94
    risk-averse and risk-hungry 27
cybernetics 39
cycle
    decision 29–30, 31–59
    feedback 39–40
    learning 13, 23, 91, 111

debate 68
decisions
    categories 10–11
    context of 10, 18, 23–8, 111
    definition of 15–16
    evaluating 59
    ownership of 24–6, 28
    parameters of 10
    'point of no return' 9, 16, 83
    reviewing 12, 23, 111, 124–30,
        132
    'selling' 98–103
decision making 22–3
    decision cycle 29–30, 31–59
    designing solutions 22–3, 31, 59,
        91
    managing 28–30
    prejudices about 17, 50
    styles of 9, 12, 56–7, 62–4
    systematic approach 29
    in teams 73–8
delegation 103–8
    how to delegate 106–8
    what to delegate 104–5
Deming, W Edwards 66

development, staff 130–3
Drucker, P 68, 83

empowerment 63
engagement, principle of 89–90
enquiry
    and advocacy, balancing 70–2
excursion, metaphorical 47

Failure Prevention Analysis 82–3
fears
    coping strategies 86–7
    recognizing 85–6
fishbone diagrams 38–9
Flesch, R 98
Force Field Analysis 57, 96–7
Fritz, R 86

goals, sharing 108–10
    goal support grid 109–10
groupthink 74, 79

Harvard Business Review 68
hats, thinking (de Bono) 72–3
Honey, P 130
'how/how' thinking 48–9
'how to' 42–5

incubation 88
inference, ladder of (Argyris) 70–2
information
    gathering 18, 46–7, 73, 111
    presenting 101
intuition 12, 13, 20–1, 50, 73
    developing 87–9
Ishikawa, Prof. K 38
    diagrams 38–9

Jung, C G 20–1

Kepner-Tregoe method 10

Keynes J M 47
key result areas 112, 113, 115, 116, 118, 124

ladder of inference 70–2
leadership 117
learning cycle 13, 23, 91, 111

meetings
  brainstorming 77–8
  performance review 126–8
  presenting at 102
  team 75–6, 121–4, 126–8
  team briefing 103
metaphorical excursion 47
mindsets 47
Murray W H 90

Neumann, J von 23
Nicholaidis, N 56

objectives
  of conversations 66
  definition 118
  of meetings 75, 121
  range, extending 44–5
  reviewing 83, 87
  setting 38, 107, 112, 115, 116, 124
  supporting 109
opinions 68
oracle, using 48
Osborn, A 97

Pareto Analysis 34–6
Pasteur, L 88
Pepys, S 45
performance, monitoring 112, 116–17, 124–30
  indicators 113, 116, 118
  one-to-ones 125–6
  resistance to, overcoming 121–4

review 115–17, 121–2
  team review 126–8
Peter, L J 112
Prai-Barshana 77
presentations 101–3
probability, calculating 52–3, 81, 82–3
problems
  constructed 41–5
  identifying 32–3, 37–8
  presented 36–41
  structure of 34
  types 11
problem solving 11, 16
  backwards planning 43–4
  'how to' 42–3
  incubation 88
  problem statement 33

Ranking and Rating 13, 51–2, 56
report writing 100–1
Rickards, Tudor 11
risk 81, 91
  emotional, managing 83–7
  objective, managing 81–3
  and organizational culture 27
  and reward balancing 53
rule reversal 47

Schmidt, W 62
Senge, P 24, 39, 41, 65
Sloan, A 87
Snyder, R 68
solutions, designing 22–3, 31, 59, 91
Solution Effect Analysis 13, 54, 56
Sperry, R 12
spheres of influence 66, 94–5
'sponsors' 94–5
  gaining 95
systems thinking 23–4, 39–41

feedback cycles 39–40
and force field analysis 96–7
leverage 41

Tannenbaum, R 62
targets 112, 113, 114–15, 116, 118,
    125–6
definition 119
and objectives 124
reviewing 124–5
setting 119–21, 124, 126
team briefing 103
teamwork 63
advantages 73–4
to consult 73–8, 80
dangers 74, 79–80
meetings 75–6, 121–4

thinking 12, 17–19
adversarial 68–9
ego 69
and enquiry 70
hats, six (de Bono) 72–3
making visible 71–2
political 69
range, increasing 72–3
rigid 69
Townsend, R 24
TQM 13
training 108, 116, 130, 132

walking the job 128–30
Wallaczek, M 67, 106
Watson, T J 91
Weiler A H 106